EXPLOSIVE POWER ON TRAMWAYS IN THE BRITISH ISLES

THE STORY OF TRAMWAYS USING

INTERNAL COMBUSTION ENGINES

By David Voice

Published by Adam Gordon

ALSO BY DAVID VOICE

How to Go Tram and Tramway Modelling, 3 editions
London's Tramways Their History and How to Model Them
What Colour Was That Tram?
Tramway Modelling in 'OO' Gauge
More Tramway Modelling in 'OO' Gauge
The Illustrated History of Kidderminster and Stourport Electric Tramway (with Melvyn Thompson)
The Millennium guide to Trams in the British Isles
The Definitive Guide to Trams in the British Isles
Toy and Model Trams of the World, Volumes 1 & 2 (with Gottfried Kuře)
Next Stop Seaton! 3 editions (with David Jay)
Hospital Tramways and Railways, 3 editions
Freight on Street Tramways in the British Isles
British Tramcar Manufacturers, British Westinghouse and Metropolitan-Vickers
Works Tramcars of the British Isles
The Age of the Horse Tram
Monorails of the World
Tram and Bus Tokens of the British Isles
Battery Trams of the British Isles
Mono-Rail, The History of the industrial monorails made by Road Machines Ltd, Metalair Ltd, and Rail Machines Ltd
Tramway Reflections
Shocking Solutions to a Current Problem
Seaton Tramway – It's Electric
Seaton Tramway – The Valentine's Day Storm
The History of Worcester's Tramways
Last Rides - Funeral Trams Around the World
All Dressed Up and Somewhere to Go, the History of Decorated Tramcars in the British Isles
Slot Machines, The History of Cable Hauled Street Tramways in the British Isles
Kidderminster and Stourport Electric Tramway Company Ltd.

A catalogue entry for this book is available from the British Library

ISBN 978-1-910654-15-6
Publication no. 119
Published in 2017 by Adam Gordon, Kintradwell Farmhouse, Brora, Sutherland KW9 6LU
Tel: 01408 622660

Printed by 4Edge Ltd, Hockley, Essex SS5 4AD

EXPLOSIVE POWER
ON TRAMWAYS IN THE BRITISH ISLES

CONTENTS

The first gas tramcar to be delivered to the Lytham St Annes Tramway.

FOREWORD

All my life I have tended to be interested in the slightly more obscure aspects of the history of British tramways. Researching these less documented aspects has led me through fascinating times where I have discovered unusual information, often in less obvious places. The subject of this book has been one of the most challenging of all the themes I have explored. Tramway vehicles powered by internal combustion engines and running on rails have tended to be ignored by most tram enthusiasts. I always expect that some of the earlier history of tramways, where the events happened over 100 years ago, is likely to be difficult to find and I found this to be very true in this instance. There was an additional complication as I had difficulty determining what to include and what to omit. Clearly, any vehicle that ran on tram rails (i.e. was guided by the rails) and was powered by an internal combustion engine needed to be in the book. The difficulty came when considering those vehicles that only had road wheels, but that provided direct services to the tramway. The prime example of this type of vehicle was the overhead repair lorry. When involved in their principal duties, they fall outside the scope of this book. However, it is most likely that the majority were also used to tow unserviceable trams back to the depot (most tramways had an overhead repair lorry, few had dedicated breakdown lorries). To complicate the matter, any records of such uses disappeared many years ago (if indeed they were ever kept). The only records are if, by chance, someone happened to take a photograph of the event. Such records, alas, give no indication of the frequency of such uses. I decided not to second guess whether any particular system used their overhead lorries as breakdown vehicles, and I have only included those where I have found clear evidence. I realise that some readers may disagree with my choice, but this is something that makes the subject more interesting.

I was surprised that finding information on ancillary vehicles even for those tramways currently operating, has also proved difficult. There is plenty of information and photographs about the passenger vehicles. However, there are other vehicles where data is less easy to discover. Frequently fleet lists will ignore non-passenger vehicles. Indeed, one type of vehicle is routinely ignored, the road-rail ancillary engineer's lorry. The common use of vehicles that can operate on both roads and rails is relatively new. Quite clearly these have proved to be invaluable to modern tramways, yet they are largely ignored by enthusiasts. Frequently they are tucked away at the back of depot buildings and only come out for emergencies or when the tramway is not operating, usually at night. So they are generally not on public view. There has also been a trend to contract out much infrastructure repair and development work. In these cases, the contractor provides their own road-rail vehicles that appear just for the specific contract and then disappear. Often working on right-of-way sections they manage to keep away from enthusiasts' cameras and may not appear on any records of the tramway. I hope I have been able to identify all of those vehicles that are (or at some time were) owned by British tramways and in some cases those contractors' vehicles that spent significant periods on one tramway. However, I admit that the record of contractors' vehicles may be sporadic.

I have also discovered that tramway operators will give much publicity to new passenger tramcars that are added to their fleets. However, they are far less likely to make any announcement or give any publicity for their ancillary vehicles. In one case a second-hand diesel locomotive was purchased by a museum to be used as a source of spares. The acquisition was never made public and the vehicle stayed in a store for years. Its existence only came to light when it was moved to the main depot to be broken up for scrap. There were similar difficulties of finding information when an ancillary vehicle was no longer required and it was sold on. In some situations, it was impossible to find the fate of the vehicle. It may have been sold on to another tramway, or to a business with no connections with tramways or broken up for scrap. In a number of cases I discovered what happened to certain vehicles only by the kindness of friends sharing information with me or by my accidentally coming across a mention of them. I must also make reference to the acknowledgements page. I owe a deep gratitude to all those who have generously provided information and patiently answered my questions about obscure vehicles and systems.

NOTE
The dates given in the headings for each entry are the dates during which internal combustion vehicles were used on that tramway. They are not the dates the tramway opened and closed.

CHAPTER 1

INTRODUCTION

SEEKING A MORE EFFECTIVE POWER

After the initial enthusiasm for horse tramways, and then the realisation that they were far from the path to untold riches that was initially believed, horse tramway proprietors sought ways to increase profits. One way was to reduce costs, and the most expensive of all the costs were the horses. Unlike the human employees, horses could only work a few hours a day. To try to get more from them risked seeing them collapse in the street and shorten their working life. So each tramcar had one crew per day, but three or more sets of horses. Also if the crew did not turn up for work they did not get paid, but sick horses not only continued to need feeding, but incurred vets' bill as well.

So the search was on for an alternative, and cheaper, source of power. This was the late 1800s, when all kinds of powered machines were being developed and it was not clear which would be suitable for tramway use. Steam locomotives had been increasingly used on railways from the early trials and demonstrations dating from the early 1800s. By the 1870s steam tram locomotives were being used on road tramways. However, they were subject to strict limitations set by Parliament, and trams carried small numbers of passengers (compared to railway trains), stopped very frequently and mixed with other road traffic. These limitations meant that steam was almost as expensive as horses.

So the search for other types of power continued. This included some ideas that are familiar to us and some that appear rather strange. In the latter are clockwork, compressed air and wind (using ship-like sails). Slightly more successful were cable hauled, internal combustion, and steam tramways, while the most successful was electricity. The histories of most of these different power sources have been extensively written; however, one has been relatively ignored and that is the internal combustion engine. I hope to remedy that deficiency with this book.

INTERNAL COMBUSTION ENGINES

The first internal combustion engines were being developed in the 1790s and some used gas and others used volatile liquids as the fuel. Experiments continued for many years and it was not until the 1820s that internal combustion engines started to be used commercially. The four stroke compression engine was not patented until 1876 by Nikolaus Otto and others. However, German courts ruled that the four stroke cycle could not be patented and so others were free to use it. Among these was Karl Benz. He was also granted the first patent for an internal combustion engine powered automobile in 1886.

GAS TRAMCARS

The first recorded use of an internal combustion engine in a tramcar is in 1886 on a tramline running from Alphington to Clifton Hill, both in the northern part of Melbourne. The tramcar has been described as using naptha gas or town (coal) gas. The tramcar itself was said to have originated as a 40 seat railway carriage that had a gas engine fitted. The tram line joining the two districts was two miles long. A description of the car that was published some forty years later said that the gas engine was made by John Banks and Son and it was mounted to one side of the tramcar, driving a large flywheel. The position of the engine resulted in the vehicle rocking when the engine was operating. The tramcar appears to have been a limited success as it ran for just two years, the service being closed in 1888.

1886 also saw an article in the San Francisco Bulletin describing a gas tram being trialled in the city that was built by a Mr Noble. The tramcar was described as being similar in size and shape

Before the first gas trams started running in Lytham St Anne's in 1896 they had been tried out in several German cities, including this car that ran in Berlin.

as the cable grip cars. The experimental car appears not to have any provision for passengers as the report says that later there would be 20 seats added. The article lacks detail about the power source. It says that there was a gas engine powered by gas held in a reservoir that was re-charged once a day using a rubber tube. This implies that it was town gas that was used. Howev-er, there is a description that the gas engine powered a dynamo to generate electricity to light the tramcar and provide power to drive the engine on steep grades and when starting. The gas en-gine was said to operate continuously, even when the car was stationary.

Over time two types of car were developed using gas as their power source:

Gas-Electric (G-E) was the system used in the first experimental gas powered tramcars. The gas engine drove a generator and the electricity then powered motors turning the wheels. No tram of this type is thought to have been operated in Britain.

Gas-Mechanical (G-M) This was the method used by the British Gas Traction Company where the gas engine drove a large flywheel that was continuously rotated. The energy in the flywheel was used to drive the car through clutches and gearboxes.

PETROL TRAMCARS

In Britain, the first thoughts of using petrol engines to power tramcars came in 1896 when the Daimler Motor Car Company took a stand at the Imperial Institute Exhibition to advertise their petrol motors including a narrow gauge tramcar. As a more practical demonstration of petrol-mechanical tramcars, the Sidney Straker and Squire Limited Company supplied petrol tramcars to carry visitors on a tramway built around the site. They were promoting their new narrow gauge petrol tramcar driven by a similar petrol engine that they used in their motor cars, except the tramcar had two cylinders (the motor car engine was single cylinder). The single deck vehicle had knifeboard seating in an open tramcar with a light roof. It was clearly aimed at the overseas

**One of the four petrol tramcars made by McEwan Pratt and Company in 1920
for the Nashik Tramways, India.**

market where the weather was much warmer than Britain. The engine drove one axle through a two speed gearbox. However, no reference to any sales of these items has been found.

Subsequently further types of petrol powered tram vehicles were developed. These were:

Petrol-Mechanical (P-M) where a petrol engine drives the wheels of the vehicle through a conventional clutch and gearbox.

Petrol-Electric (P-E) where the petrol engine drives a generator that in turn powers electric motors attached to the axles of the vehicle. The control is accomplished through an electric controller. This type was used where a tramcar had conventional electric motors that worked from the overhead supply or from the power generated on board.

Petrol-Hydraulic (P-H) where the petrol engine drives a hydraulic pump that is used to energise hydraulic power units on the axles.

DIESEL TRAMCARS

In the 1890s Rudolf Diesel started developing his compression ignition engine. The diesel differed from the petrol engine as it did not require the fuel to be ignited by a spark. The compression stage of the cycle created so much pressure in the air that it heated sufficiently to ignite the fuel when it was injected into the cylinder at the top of the compression stroke. What Diesel was seeking was a more efficient use of fuel. Steam engines, particularly the early examples, were very inefficient, only converting around 10% of the fuel energy into mechanical motion. The petrol engine was better at around 20%, though still losing most of its fuel energy. The first diesel engines had an efficiency of around 30%.

Rudolf Diesel died in 1913 in mysterious circumstances. He was travelling by ferry from Antwerp to England to meet with the British Navy to discuss using diesel engines in submarines (at the time petrol engines were favoured but their inefficiency meant the range of the vessels was very limited). On the journey he fell overboard and was drowned. There has been much speculation about the events of that day. Did he fall, was he pushed or did he jump? There has been much conjecture, with conspiracy theories abounding. However, he was in severe financial difficulty and most people feel that he took his own life. His invention had proved his ideas were sound and he had produced the most efficient engine that became the workhorse of the industrial world.

As far as tramcars were concerned there were three main types of drive developed, basically the same as the petrol engine, but substituting a diesel engine power unit:

Diesel-Mechanical (D-M)

Diesel-Electric (D-E)

Diesel-Hydraulic (D-H)

The Clogher Valley Railway had one diesel passenger coach built in 1932 now an exhibit in the Ulster Folk and Transport Museum.

OTHER FUELS

When the Castleberg and Victoria Bridge Tramway wanted to reduce costs they built their own paraffin powered railcar. It is believed to have been the only railed tramway vehicle in the British Isles to be powered by paraffin.

In the early days of internal combustion engines, the fuels used were sometimes slightly different from the diesel, petrol and paraffin that we are so familiar with today. In 1893 the Connelly tramway locomotive used mineral oil as its fuel, using an early form of internal combustion engine fuel.

The Daimler Motor Car Company built an experimental railed vehicle in 1896 that was fuelled with oil or benzoline (benzole is a derivative similar to petroleum but sourced from coal-tar). It was not a success.

MORE MODERN DEVELOPMENTS

None of the modern generation of passenger tramcars use internal combustion (I/C) engines. However, I/C has carved a niche for itself in ancillary support vehicles. Wholly railed vehicles are used by modern tramways as they often have significant lengths of private right of way with open trackwork. By using I/C power, ancillary vehicles are able to travel when the overhead loses power, either when engineers are working on it or when there has been an accident damaging the wires. In recent years there has been the development of more versatile ancillary vehicles, the adaptation of road lorries to be able to run on rails. There are two types currently in use. Both use rubber tyres in the normal manner for road use, but they differ when travelling on rails. The most common type makes use of the road drive. Small metal flanged wheels are lowered to run on the rails, while allowing the tyres to run along the top of the rails. The friction between the tyre and the rail enables the lorry to be driven along the top of the rails while the flanged wheels keep the vehicle on the rails. The other type makes more use of the small metal flanged wheels. They are lowered sufficiently to raise the road wheels off the rails. The drive is accomplished through the metal flanged wheels.

The advantage of these vehicles is very apparent. They can travel to problems using the public highway. If necessary, they can then run onto the rails and travel on private rights of way. If the problem is an unserviceable tramcar, the maintenance vehicle can overtake other tramcars delayed by the hold-up and get to the stricken car. Not surprisingly these road-rail works lorries have proved extremely popular, and useful, to modern systems.

A contractor's road-rail vehicle parked on the Snow Hill stop of the Midland Metro when it was the terminus.

CHAPTER 2

GAS TRAMS IN BRITAIN

CONNELLY OIL MOTOR 1893

In 1893 the Connelly Oil Motor was trialled on the London, Deptford and Greenwich Tramways and the Croydon and Thornton Heath Tramway Company lines. Fuelled by mineral oil (a derivative of petroleum) it resembled a steam tram dummy locomotive, as it did not carry passengers, but hauled a horse tramcar. The trials in Croydon took place in July 1893 on a route that went from Poplar Walk to the Thornton Heath terminus. The only photograph of the vehicle shows it hauling an Aldgate and Stratford Tramway tramcar, though there is no record of the Connelly car being used on that tramway.

The only known photograph of the Connelley Oil Motor Locomotive. It is hauling a North Metropolitan tramcar from the Aldgate and Stratford route (though there is no record of it having run anywhere except the London, Deptford and Greenwich Tramways and the Croydon and Thornton Heath Tramway).

The engine ran at a constant speed and so to drive the car a small friction wheel ran on a metal disc that was rotated by the engine. Moving the friction wheel across the disc gave effectively an infinitely variable drive. When still, the friction wheel was at the centre of the disc, but raised slightly away from it. On starting it was lowered onto the disc and moved slightly from the centre, thus being rotated and driving the wheels of the tramcar. A separate gear box with a clutch was provided to allow the car to be driven in either direction. The efficiency (or lack of) was illustrated by the oil consumption where over 70 gallons of fuel was used to travel 500 miles. It was said to be capable of travelling at the Board of Trade maximum speed limit of eight miles per hour.

CROYDON GAS TRAM EXPERIMENT 1893 - 1894

In October 1893 the Traction Syndicate Limited agreed with the Croydon and Thornton Heath Tramways Company for it to carry out trials of their Lührig designed tramcar. The design had been given trials in Dresden and Dessau and the patents had been acquired by the Traction Syndicate Limited. It first ran on March 15th 1894. The tramcar was designed by Carl Lührig, was improved by Mr Holt of Crossley Brothers and built in Dresden by the Carl Stoll Company. The Dresden tramway had five such tramcars operating on their tramway. It was powered by an Otto gas engine built by Deutz that had two opposing cylinders driving a crankshaft and fitted under the longitudinal seat on one side of the lower saloon, with a large flywheel using space behind the seat back. The gas was held in three tanks, one under the other seat and two fitted transversely under the chassis. The cylinders could hold thirty-five cubic ft. of gas that was supplied at 120 lbs per cu. in. (8 atmospheres) pressure. This was sufficient to power the tramcar for a journey of eight to ten miles and provide gas lighting in the car. The gas drawn into the engine was ignited by an electric spark (using a battery on the tramcar) and the pistons drove the crankshaft. A large flywheel was fitted to the shaft. The shaft drove a two speed gear box which was connected to one axle by chain drives via friction clutches. A lever allowed the direction of travel to be reversed, the controls being at both ends of the car. The tramcar was single deck, weighing 5½ tons and 18ft. long overall, the body being 11ft. long. It was capable of carrying twenty-eight passengers.

When idling, the motor fired just one cylinder, once on every eighth revolution, the engine being kept rotating by the four ft. diameter flywheel. The single deck tramcar could carry 14 passengers in the saloon and six on each platform. The car was inspected by General Hutchinson, of the Board of Trade. He required modifications to be made prior to the start of any trials.

A charging station was built at the tramway Company's Thornton Heath depot, where an 8hp Otto engine drove a Pintsch gas pump. The gas supply was taken from the town gas mains and was pumped into a large cylinder, 25ft. long by 4ft. diameter, at 150 lbs. per sq. in. (10 atmospheres). The tramcar was charged in two minutes using a rubber hose from a stand-pipe. The engine of the car ran continuously, the drive being disengaged when the car was stationary. At such times the supply of gas to one cylinder ceased and the engine ran using just one cylinder. The top speed of the car was limited by the Board of Trade to 8 mph and the cost of gas was found to be 1d per mile compared to 3½d – 4d per mile for feeding and keeping horses.

The second tramcar also had a two-cylinder Otto gas engine fed under eight atmospheres pressure from three reservoirs, the principal being located longitudinally under one of the seats. It was claimed to be able to run from eight to ten miles at one charge of town gas. The gas, from the normal town supply, was held in a reservoir under pressure and refilled between trips. Again the two-cylinder motor ran continuously with a large flywheel being used to even out the power strokes of the Otto engine. The direct drive to the wheels was undertaken through a clutch and two speed gear box, plus a reversing mechanism. In May 1894 General Hutchinson was back inspecting a second Lührig car and again he allowed the car to run for six months.

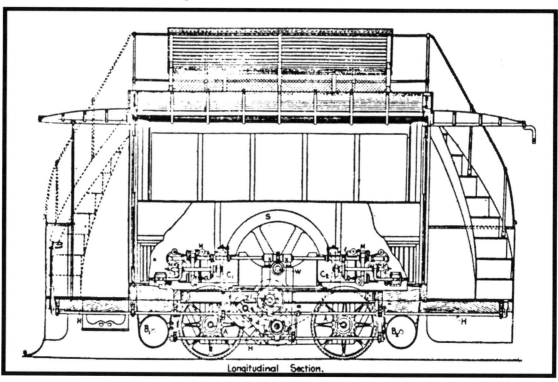

Longitudinal Section.

Drawing of the Lührig Gas Tramcar, similar to the Croydon car, but the trial in Croydon used single deck tramcars.

It was described as "not noticeably different from a horse car, it runs quietly and easily, emitting neither smoke nor steam, and it is quite under control". An advantage that was emphasised by the Gas Traction Company was that there was no soot (a disadvantage of steam trams), smoke, noise, vibration, or smell. The Traction Syndicate Limited hoped that the tramway would soon have five such trams with another five to be added later. Optimistically they stated that it was intended that the gas cars would entirely supersede the horse cars on the Croydon and Thornton

Heath Tramway Company's system a forecast that was not fulfilled and the history of this tramcar in Britain ends here. There is no record of the subsequent life of the car except for an oblique mention in The Engineer for 28th July 1899. The tramway continued to operate as a horse tramway until conversion to electric power. A glimpse into what may have happened is given in the history of the Dresden tramcars. It was found that the prediction for the distance available between charges was over optimistic. The trams needed recharging after every journey, with passengers having to wait considerably more than the suggested two minutes. Passengers also complained of the unpleasant smell of the gas and the potential hazard from explosions. The latter was realised in December 1894 when there was an explosion while the gas tank was being refilled. The Dresden gas trams were in service for just two years, 1894 to 1896. They were sold to Dessau where they operated until withdrawal in 1901 when that system was electrified.

SHIPLEY GLEN TRAMWAY 1895 - 1928

A fairground was built along Prod Lane, a road on the ridge along the top of Shipley Glen, West Yorkshire, that had a number of entertaining rides. A local entrepreneur, Sam Wilson, realised that people would find it easier to visit the fairground if they could be conveyed up the steep slope of the Glen. In 1895 he built a funicular, that he called a tramway, that opened on 18th May. It had a dual purpose, firstly saving people the vigorous walk up the side of the Glen and the other as an entertaining ride of its own. Being a funicular it is debatable if this line should be included in this book. However, my interests tend to be broad and I have included it, even though some may disagree.

The original cars that ran from the opening of the funicular in 1865 to around 1912 when they were replaced by the cars currently in use. The original cars were operated by the gas engine, which was converted to paraffin some years before the old cars were replaced.

The short line is a true funicular with two passenger trams, each with two cars with crossbench seating. A cable connects the trains and the line was originally powered by a 8hp gas motor, located at the top of the line. The motor powered a winch that raised and lowered the cars. It was operated from a control room situated at the top station. As the tramway was somewhat remote, there was no connection to town gas, so the tramway produced its own gas. Anthracite was burnt to produce the gas, though the smell was described as 'dreadful'. Later town gas was supplied from a pipe connected to the Salts Mills Building, Saltaire. In 1915 the motor was converted to run on paraffin and it ran in this condition until 1928, when it was replaced by an electric motor.

The first electric motor continued service for almost forty years. Unfortunately the tramway was closed for a short while in 1967 and during this time the structure and electric motor were vandalized. When the tramway was restored, a new electric motor was fitted and this continues to power the tramway. If visiting the tramway make sure you pop into the small museum at the lower terminus.

LYTHAM ST ANNES GAS TRAMS 1896 - 1903

In 1885 an electric tramway was opened along the Blackpool promenade, the first tramway on the mainland to be powered by electricity. The Corporation would not allow the use of an overhead wire supply, as it would detract from the beauty of the sea front. So the tramway chose to use the conduit system, despite the problems of ingress by sea water and sand. Lytham St Annes clearly felt that they should keep up with their neighbour and the Blackpool St Annes and Lytham Tramways Company was established in 1893 following the passing of the Blackpool St Annes and Lytham Tramways Act. However, the Council insisted that the Act should prohibit the use of steam or cable on the tramway. Unfortunately, there is no surviving record of the reason for choosing gas trams. One of the contemporaneous magazines commented "The idea of gas traction is absolutely new to England, though it has been well tested in Germany, there being three systems at Dresden, Berlin, and Dessau, and the cars have run since the inception of gas traction three hundred and fifty thousand miles with the greatest success".

A very relaxed photograph. Note all the ladies and children are in the lower saloon. The lower part of the flywheel cover is clearly seen below the company crest.

The section of the line within its boundary was built by Blackpool Corporation and the remainder, in St Annes and Lytham, was built by the tramway Company. The initial section of the line was opened in 1896 with four gas powered tramcars to the Lührig design of the Gas Traction Company of London and Dresden. The mechanical operation of the tramcars was similar to that described above for the experimental car in Croydon. However, the bodies of the cars were double deck, seating 40 (16 inside and 24 outside) and weighing 7½ tons, built by the Ashbury Railway Carriage & Iron Co. The gas engines were 14 horse power and like the experimental Croydon car were fitted under the seats on one side of the tram. The large flywheel used the space behind the other seat and below the car body. The engine normally ran at 260 rpm when being driven, while when the tram was stationary the engine was slowed to 75 rpm to save fuel. To change the direction of travel the drive was moved from one axle to the other using clutches and a gearbox. The town gas was supplied by the Lytham Council and a portable compressing plant comprising a gas engine driving a compressing pump, which filled two large Pintsch gas receivers at a pressure of about 150 lb per sq. in. The cost of the compressing unit was £350.

The operation of the tramway was leased in 1896 to the British Gas Traction Company for seven years , who operated the tramcars, the gas charging equipment and the drivers for a cost of 4½d per car mile. The contract specified that the cars should be run a minimum total of 163,000 miles per annum. The tramway Company provided the conductors and collected the fares. In the lower gear the tramcar ran at about 4 mph while in top gear the speed was 8½ mph. The Gas Traction Company was still claiming a range of eight miles between recharging, which was now being said to take one minute. In 1896 car number 4 went to Paris to demonstrate the system. No

The first four gas tramcars (1—4), purchased for Lytham in 1896, were small. A further 16 larger cars (5—20) were acquired in 1897, giving a final fleet of 20 gas cars. All were replaced by electric tramcars in 1903.

doubt the Traction Company was hoping that the Paris tramway would be persuaded to buy the cars to replace their existing Serpollet steam tramcars, however, nothing came of this.

On 11th July 1896 representatives from local authorities and the technical press were invited to the inauguration of the first four-mile section of the tramway, from the station to St Annes. A large party attended and they were met at Blackpool South Shore Station and carried in three of the four tramcars over the four miles of available track. A luncheon was held during the afternoon at the Clifton Arms Hotel, Lytham during which a number of speeches were made in support of the new tramway.

The damage incurred when the depot suffered a gale on 27th February 1903 gives an opportunity to see the large flywheel that was an essential part of the mechanism.

The tramway was successful and the Gas Company soon commissioned 16 more tramcars, to the same basic design. These were built by the Lancaster Carriage and Wagon Company in 1897 and were both more powerful (with 14 horse power motors) and had a greater capacity, being able to carry 52 passengers (22 inside and 30 outside). However, limitations soon started to become apparent. The distance travelled between recharging was found to be far below the eight miles stated by the Gas Company. The trams had to be recharged with gas twice on the route between Blackpool South Shore station and Lytham. There were two railway bridges on the route and passengers were often asked to exit the car and help push the tramcar over the bridge. As the tram line ended at South Shore Station, passengers for the centre of Blackpool had to wait for a Blackpool Corporation tramcar to take them for the remainder of the journey. Unfortunately for the tramway there was a railway service that took passengers directly between the centres of the two towns.

In 1898 the Blackpool tramway was improved when a new route was opened that had an overhead electrical supply, rather than the unreliable conduit. In the same year the Lytham tramway became a public Company, issuing 85,000 shares. This capital was used to buy out the British Gas Company's contract, thus freeing the tramway from the obligation to use gas trams. The gas charging equipment and depot were moved to within the Blackpool Corporation boundary, where the cost of town gas was cheaper. By now it was found that the demand during the summer holidays outstripped the number of trams available, so second-hand horse trams were purchased and used alongside the gas cars. In 1900 the tramway Company applied for and obtained an Act to convert the system to electric operation and double most of the track. With the prospect of electric operation, the Electric Tramways Construction and Maintenance Company Ltd. purchased the Lytham tramway. Electrifying the line began at the end of 1902. The end of the gas trams was hastened in February 1903 when the Lytham depot and its 13 trams were damaged by a gale. Although 7 trams did survive in a smaller depot, the gas trams never entered passenger service again, though they were used as works vehicles during the conversion of the tramway. The electric tramway was opened in May 1903. Some of the original four smaller cars and the 16 larger cars (some damaged) were sold to Neath, others had a less usual retirement, the lower saloon of at least one becoming the home for a gypsy fortune teller.

T.P.D.S. PARIS 1896

The British Gas Traction Company was looking to open up markets for its gas trams. At this time the tramways in Paris were looking for a more economic means of traction to replace the horses. In 1896 the British Gas Traction Company offered to demonstrate their gas tramcars to the city. As mentioned above, tram number 4 was taken to Paris. It is likely that this tram was delivered directly to Paris from the manufacturing factory. It was given trials on the Compagnie des Tramways de Paris et du Département de la Seine line from the gas works at Landy to the Port de Saint-Ouen. It would appear that the tests were disappointing as the experiment was short-lived and the tramcar returned to Britain.

A poor, but rare, photograph of the Lytham St Annes gas tramcar under trial on the Paris tramways. It is by the Saint-Ouen Town Hall. As can be seen it was not allowed to carry the public and the visit was short. Presumably the tramway company was not impressed by performance of the tram.

DAIMLER MOTOR CAR COMPANY OIL TRAMCAR 1896

Among the exhibits at the Imperial Institute Exhibition (London's first Motor Show) was an example of a petrol-mechanical narrow gauge tramcar built by the Daimler Motor Car Company. It had a two-cylinder engine, powered using oil or benzoline (benzole, a derivative similar to petroleum but sourced from coal-tar). The engine drove one axle through a clutch and two speed gearbox. The four-wheel vehicle had longitudinal seating for the passengers. It was open sided and had a light roof, clearly designed for warm climes. No further mention has been found of this tramcar. It is assumed that the Daimler Motor Company had such success with the automobiles that it had no need to continue with tramcars.

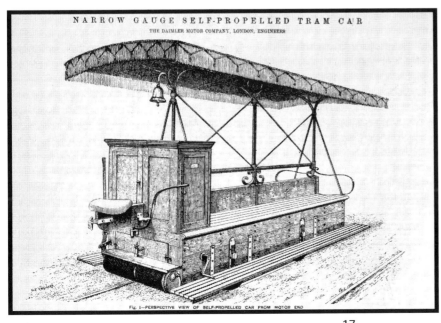

The simple open-sided oil powered Daimler tramcar, clearly aimed at countries with a warm climate.

TRAFFORD PARK GAS TRAMS 1897 - 1908

Trafford Hall, occupied by the Trafford family, dated back to the 14th century and was surrounded by over 700 acres of the Trafford Park Estates. The industrialisation of Manchester saw the building of the Bridgewater Canal in 1759 to improve communication, particularly to transport coal from the Duke of Bridgewater's mines in Worsley. Part of the canal went through the Trafford Park Estate. As Manchester expanded, a better way to distribute goods was needed and in 1882 a group of businessmen proposed the Manchester Ship Canal. It took three years to get an Act through Parliament and a further nine before the canal was completed and opened in 1894. The then owner of Trafford Hall was planning to leave and, as the new canal went close to the hall, he decided to sell the estate. This took a while and finally a businessman purchased it and set up the Trafford Park Estates Company. The Company opened a golf course and used the hall as a hotel, soon becoming the club house for the golf club. Meanwhile other areas of the estate were used for factories. The estates Company realised that some form of passenger transport was needed in the park. One of the Directors of the estates Company had read about the Blackpool, St Annes and Lytham tramway and suggested that gas trams could be the answer. The Directors contacted the British Gas Traction Company and were impressed with the use of gas trams. It was agreed that the estates Company would lay three miles of tramway track through the estate and the traction Company would operate the gas tramway. It was intended that there would be six tramcars, though only four were ever ordered. They were commissioned from the Lancaster Carriage and Wagon Company and appear to be to the same design as the second batch of cars built for the Lytham tramway.

From 1897 the Trafford Park Tramway had four gas tramcars that provided service until 1908 by which time the tramcars had reached the end of their working life. The gas tramway closed and the tramcars were scrapped.

The estates Company started laying the track and announced that the tramway would be opening for the Royal Agricultural Show in June 1897. However, this was not to be. The traction Company needed to know the frequency of service to arrange for an adequate gas supply (town gas supplied by Salford Corporation) and details of the rail profile and depot design. But in the haste to get everything ready for the celebrations for the show, the traction Company was ignored. A temporary railway steam goods service started using part of the track, though not enough attention

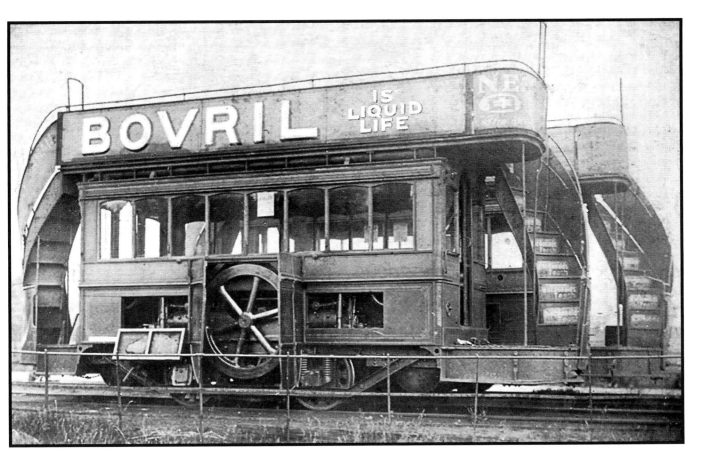

The gas tramcar with its inspection panels opened, showing the pistons either side of the flywheel.

was paid to the difference between the wheel profiles of railways and tramways. The traction Company was also very worried at the poor quality of track laying. This brought them into conflict with the building contractor, Marshall Stevens, and the estates Company Manager, also Marshall Stevens. On the opening date the traction Company considered that the track was not ready and to hold the opening ceremony on 4th June 1897 the guests were taken for a trip in railway trucks and told that the opening of the tramway was delayed for a week. The Secretary of the traction Company visited the site and was appalled by what he found. The depot and recharging machinery were far from being completed, the gas mains had yet to be laid and the track was in an unacceptable state.

One tramcar was delivered to the Park on 21st June 1897 and, to placate Marshall Stevens, the traction Company Manager took it out on a test run, which was successful. The next day he took Marshall Stevens on a trial trip after which several more trips were made. It was agreed that the tramway could open to the public the next day Friday 23rd July. Trips were made until the sixth day when the tramcar derailed, injuring two lady passengers in the lower saloon. The Estates Manager argued for the tramway to re-open, but the traction Company was more prudent and stopped the service until an investigation into the reason for the derailment was undertaken. An independent inspection reported that the track had been very badly laid. The cause of the derailment was that the points had not been laid correctly and did not accept the narrower wheels of the tramcars. The argument continued and the line lay idle while each party tried to persuade the other to take action to rectify the issue. The dispute continued to 8th April 1898 when the tramway service finally re-opened with three additional cars being delivered, bringing the fleet to four.

The tramcars were, as far as can be determined, manufactured to the same specification as the second batch of tramcars made for the Lytham tramway. The bodies were made by the Lancaster Carriage and Wagon Company and the mechanical elements were described as being the same as the previous cars. One additional insight into the tramcars was the nickname they quickly gained of "Lamp Oil Express" that described the smell of the engines when they were working.

The tramway operated for another year by which time the British Gas Traction Company was in serious financial difficulty. They wrote to the estates Company in April 1899 to inform them that the tramway service would cease from July. The estates Company managed to negotiate an extension of the gas tramway services until the end of the year, by which time the Park would have an electric supply. The trams continued to run, but the traction Company had gone into liquidation on 1st November 1899 and owed the Salford Corporation £73 14s 5d for gas, so it was cut off. Salford refused to reconnect until the bill was paid. The estates Company offered to pay the bill, but Salford refused as the Company had no control over the traction Company's affairs. The tramways ceased running on 3rd November. The only solution that was open to the estates Company was to buy the traction Company. This cost £2,000, but it meant that the estates Company could legally pay the outstanding bill and insist on reinstatement of the gas supply. The tramway reopened with the gas trams. The tramway from the Trafford Road entrance to the Post Office was converted to electric operation, which opened on 14th July 1903. This meant that the gas tram route was shortened to terminate at the Post Office. By 1907 it was clear that the four gas tramcars were reaching the end of their working life. They carried on in service, but by April 1908 only two were able to be operated. It was decided to replace the gas tramcars by a steam locomotive hauling two carriages. In June 1908 the gas tramcars and associated equipment were auctioned off. All the tramcars were sold to a local scrap merchant, though the Provincial Gas Traction Company did enquire who had purchased the tramcars as they were interested in buying some parts as spares for the tramway at Neath.

NEATH GAS TRAMS 1897 - 1920

The first tramway in Neath was a standard gauge horse drawn system that opened in 1875 with a four-mile long route from Briton Ferry, through Neath town centre to Skewen railway station. The operator was the Neath and District Tramways Company. In 1897 the Neath Corporation acquired

This is one of the larger tramcars that came second-hand from Lytham St Annes tramway in 1903. It ran until the end of the gas tramway in 1920.

The Neath depot housed an oil engine used to compress the town gas to around 150 lb per sq. in. The gas was stored in large pressure cylinders, one of which is visible at the left of the photograph.

the tramway and looking at the timing it appears that the Corporation was using its powers under the Tramway Act to compulsorily purchase the undertaking after 21 years of the operation by the private Company. The Corporation continued the horse operation while they made the decision on what the replacement should be. At this time, when most Corporations took over horse tramways in their area they chose to replace them with electric operation. However, the Neath Corporation chose to replace the horse trams with gas trams. What the reasoning was is not known, the Corporation entered into an agreement in April 1898 where the tramway would be operated by the British Gas Traction Company using gas trams. Like the second batch of trams used by Lytham and all the trams at Trafford Park, the tramcars were made by the Lancaster Railway Carriage and Wagon Company. No doubt the new trams required a more substantial track than the lighter horse tramcars. So the tram track was relaid, continuing the single track however with more passing loops. The new track was ready by October 1898, but the Traction Company had no gas trams available. Then they said that they could not use the gas trams because the Corporation had not laid the gas main to the depot, so they could not charge the tramcars, something the Corporation denied. For whatever reasons the Traction Company had to continue with a horse tram service and it was not until 31st August 1899 that the public gas tram service commenced. The service was not welcomed by everyone. The local paper commented that the tramway was very erratic with frequent stoppages and allowing school children to riding unofficially on the dashes of the cars.

This coincided with the financial difficulties of the Traction Company. The Corporation saw newspaper reports in December 1898 that the Company was in difficulties. This culminated with the notice of liquidation in November 1899. The British Electric Traction Company (BET) saw an opportunity and approached the Corporation to suggest they changed to electric operation. However, the Corporation declined to meet with them. A new company, the Traction Company of the UK Ltd., put themselves forward to take on the tramway, however, the Corporation refused. Instead the Tramway Manager, Matthew Whittington, raised local funding and with the agreement of the Corporation he formed the Provisional Gas Traction Company and at the start of 1902 took over the lease of the tramway. The Corporation was somewhat reluctant as it wanted to manage the tramway itself and the opportunity to do so came in 1916 when the Provincial Company went bankrupt. The Corporation made enquiries regarding converting to electric operation and possibly conversion to trolleybuses. During this time the gas trams continued to stagger on, with just four serviceable tramcars. All the trams were now getting old and the already high maintenance costs escalated. The Corporation stopped the tramway service in 1920, arranging for the South Wales Transport Company to provide a petrol bus service. Thus the gas tramway came to an end.

In his history of the system, Gordon Tucker concludes that the tramway initially started with eight new gas tramcars, likely to be numbered 1 – 8. They were to the same larger, 52 seat design used on the other two gas tram systems. These would be enough to work a 15 minute headway while keeping two cars as spares. The Lytham gas tramway ceased operating in 1903 and had their fleet of tramcars for sale. However, 13 of the Lytham trams had been damaged in a storm that demolished a depot. Another 7 trams survived in a second depot. It is likely that the Provisional Gas Traction Company saw an opportunity of buying extra cars and spares at a knock down price. This would have been particularly fortuitous as the British Gas Traction Company was in the throes of liquidation and in no position to provide spares or new tramcars. It is very unclear how many cars were purchased, as there is a photograph of a Lytham gas tramcar body being used as a gypsy's 'tent' on Blackpool beach. There is a photograph of Neath tramcar number 23, which suggests that the fleet had at least that number of trams and possibly a few more. However, a son of one of the tram drivers recalled that the Lytham cars retained their original numbers when they arrived at Neath, which means there may have been fewer than 23 cars, with gaps in the numbering sequence. He also recalled that only three tramcars remained in service towards the end of the tramway.

A Neath gas tramcar has survived. In 1920 Mr Frank Beddoes, who was a mechanic for the tramway, purchased the body of one of the small ex-Lytham cars to use it as a garage for his Austin Seven. He modified it by removing a bulkhead to allow access for the car and cut a door in the

One of the larger with one of the smaller tramcars in the Neath Depot

side to enable him to get out of the motor car when he parked it in the garage. In 1984 it was purchased and removed for restoration. After several years the body was renovated, but without its mechanism (it was mounted on the chassis of a railway truck). It is now on display at the Cefn Coed Colliery Museum, Crynant, South Wales, SA10 8SN.

PROPOSALS AND CONCLUSIONS

The British Gas Traction Company were keen to extend the number of tramways using their gas tramcars. News of the Lytham St Annes gas tramway was extensively publicised in the technical magazines of the time. The use of gas traction on British tramways was new and the Lytham system was a demonstration that the system worked. Towns with horse tramways became interested as the search had started for a more economic power source for the tramcars to replace the horse. One such system was Sheffield. The Corporation had taken over the horse tramway from the commercial operator and immediately set up a Committee to make recommendations on the most suitable source of power to replace the horses. They appointed a Sub Committee that visited many tramway systems in Britain and abroad. Included in their travels was a visit to the gas tramway at Lytham St Annes. A very comprehensive report was written and presented to the full Committee. The final decision was to adopt electric power using the overhead wire system. And the idea of gas traction in Sheffield was abandoned.

In May 1897, the Secretary to the British Gas Traction Company, Mr Percy Holyoake, was interviewed by the Ipswich Evening Star about the proposal to use gas tramcars on the town tramway system. He explained how the tramcars worked, the experiments in Croydon and the service at Lytham. He claimed that the Lytham gas tramcars had successfully run 40,000 miles. He also said that there was no smell from the cars, a dubious statement given the local nick name for them was "Lamp Oil Express". Subsequently nothing further was heard about the idea of the British Gas Traction Company to supply gas cars to Ipswich. When the traction Company ran into financial difficulties Mr Holyoake was appointed as liquidator of that Company.

It is fascinating to seek the reason for the failure of the gas tram. Despite the ambitious claims and the advantages of not requiring overhead wires, studs in the road or a conduit, the costs of the disadvantages outweighed these benefits. This situation was exacerbated by the lack of strong financial backing for the traction Company. Like so many innovations the initial promises were soon found to be wanting. It was soon discovered that the tramcars were very poor at climbing any sort of gradient. The cars were underpowered and even in the low gear it was not unusual for the passengers to have to push the car up hills. The smell has already been mentioned, as has the real danger of explosions occurring while refilling with gas. The major issues of the cars were their unreliability and the costs of repairing and maintaining them, made more difficult with the disappearance of spares when the British Gas Traction Company no longer traded. Having gone into liquidation in November 1899 the British Gas Traction Company continued under the management of the the liquidators until 29th August 1914 when the Company was wound up.

FURTHER READING

CONNELLY OIL MOTOR
Tramways Their Construction and Working, by D. Kinnear Clark, 1894

CROYDON
The Engineer: 22nd June 1894 p548
Tramways Their Construction and Working, by D. Kinnear Clark, 1894
Graces Guide
Tramway Review No 127: Gas Trams in Croydon – the First in Britain: by Gordon Tucker, Autumn 1986

SHIPLEY GLEN TRAMWAY
1D Up—1/2D Down, The Story of Shipley Glen and Its Tramway, by Alan Whitrick & Michael J. Leak : pub Michael Bentley 1982.

A contemporary drawing of the gas tram proposed for Ipswich. The artist has used his own interpretation to add a coupling rod between the wheels.

LYTHAM ST ANNES
The Belfast News-Letter: 13th July 1896
The Engineer: 17th July 1896 p66
The Engineer: 14th May 1897 p479
The Engineer: 21st May 1897 p479
The Engineer: 28th July 1899 p85
The Tramways of Lytham St Annes: by I. McLoughlin, J. A. Garnham, P. H. Abell: pub. Oakwood Press, 1995

T.P.D.S. PARIS
Les Tramways Parisiens: by Jean Robert, pub. G. Fuseau, 1959.

DAIMLER MOTOR COMPANY
The Engineer, 12th June 1896: Narrow Gauge Self Propelled Tram Car.

TRAFFORD PARK
The Engineer: 11th June 1897
Graces Guide
Trafford Park Tramways 1897-1946: by Edward Gray, pub. Memories, 1996

NEATH
Tramway Review Nos 107 & 108: Neath Corporation Tramways 1897-1920: by Gordon Tucker, Autumn and Winter 1981.
Tramway Review No 129: Gas Trams at Neath: Letter by J. C. Gillham, Spring 1987.

PROPOSALS AND CONCLUSIONS
The Engineer: 25th September 1896
Tramway Review No 125: Gas Trams for Ipswich?: by Edward Gray, Spring 1986
Les Tramways Parisiens: by Jean Robert, 1959.

CHAPTER 3

PETROL TRAMS IN BRITAIN

STIRLING'S MOTOR CONSTRUCTION COMPANY LIMITED 1904

The Stirling's Motor Construction Company (taken over in 1905 by the Scottish Motor Engineering Company Limited) was a Company specialising in building motor buses in their factory in Granton Harbour, Edinburgh. In 1904 they decided to expand their business by building a petrol tramcar. They were aware that the Perth tramway was seriously considering replacing their horse trams with some form of mechanisation. The Company approached Perth Council with the hope that they could sell their tramcars to the town. The major selling feature was that converting to petrol tramcars would be far less expensive than the alternatives offered by their competitors. The Company constructed a prototype car and offered to demonstrate it on the Perth tramway. The tramcar initially had an engine that was inadequate for the job and this was replaced by a 20 hp four cylinder unit. Mounted on one of the platforms the engine drove one axle through a gearbox. The weight of the car was around four tons and this proved too much for the existing horse tram track, with the tram very prone to derailment. It was found that there were many other teething difficulties and the tram was sent back to the factory for modifications, which, unfortunately, did not rectify the faults. As a result, the trial was terminated and the tramcar was returned to the factory to fade into the mists of time. It was reported in 'Commercial Motor' for January 25th 1906 that the Scottish Motor Engineering Company Limited had made a petrol tramcar as part of a larger order for an unnamed Australian tramway. I have been unable to identify which tramway it was or what happened to the tramcar.

A rather poor photograph of the Scottish Motor Engineering Company Limited petrol tramcar built in 1906 for an unknown Australian tramway.

COUNTY DONEGAL RAILWAY 1906 - 1960

It is debatable whether the County Donegal Railways should appear in a book about tramways. However, it seemed that the Irish story would remain incomplete without some reference to its contribution to the use of petrol and diesel railcars and its habit of acquiring railcars from defunct tramways. To begin, there is a very brief history of the line. It is famous as a 3ft. narrow gauge railway, however, it started life as the broad gauge (5ft. 3in.) Finn Valley Railway that opened

The first County Donegal railcar was number 1, converted in 1920 from an inspection car purchased in 1906.

between Stranorlar and Strabane in 1863. A connection was wanted between Stranorlar and Donegal, so the West Donegal Railway Company was founded to build the line. As it was expected that traffic would be limited it was decided, for economic reasons, to build the line as a 3ft. narrow gauge railway and it was opened in 1889. In 1892 the two lines merged into the Donegal Railway Company. Clearly running what should have been a continuous railway as two separate lines with different gauges was inefficient. So a first move of the new Company was to change the gauge of the old Finn Valley route to 3ft. and this was completed in 1894. New narrow gauge lines were added to the system which brought the total route mileage to 121. In 1906 the County Donegal Railways Joint Committee was established and took over from the West Donegal Railway Company.

Number 4 was the first of three petrol railcars built in the Dundalk Works. It was built in 1928, followed by numbers 5 and 6 in 1929 and 1930 respectively.

In 1906 the railway acquired a petrol driven open inspection car from Allday and Onions of Birmingham. It was the first internal combustion engine railway vehicle in Ireland. It ran in this form until 1920 when it was rebuilt with a saloon body with seating for 10 passengers and given the number 1. It proved its value during the coal strike of 1926 when it was used to carry the mail. Withdrawn in 1956, it is now an exhibit in the Ulster National Folk and Transport Museum.

Number 1 demonstrated the economies possible when using this type of vehicle, so, when the opportunity came to purchase two Ford petrol railcars from the Derwent Valley Railway, they were acquired. After being re-gauged they became numbers 2 and 3 in the Donegal fleet and they ran until being scrapped in 1934. The next three petrol railcars were built in the railway's Dundalk works. Number 4, a four wheel, 22 seat, railcar entered service in 1928, while number 5, a similar railcar but with 29 seats was built in 1929. In 1930 came number 6 that was a different design. It had seating for 32 and six wheels, a single front axle and a rear bogie. Number 4 was scrapped in 1947, number 5 lasted until 1946, while number 6 was converted into a four-wheel trailer in 1945.

Number 8, with number 7 were the first diesel powered railcars to run in regular service on any railway in the British Isles.

In 1931 railcars numbers 7 and 8 were purchased. These were ground breaking as they were the first diesel powered railcars to run in service in the British Isles. They had the same type of three axle chassis as number 6 and were equipped with Gardner diesel engines and had seats for 32 passengers. Both were withdrawn in 1949. In 1933 the railway purchased four second-hand unroadworthy buses and converted the best two into petrol railcars, becoming numbers 9 and 10. They had the more conventional four-wheel chassis with seats for 20 passengers. Number 10 was destroyed in an accidental fire in 1940, while number 9 continued in service to 1949.

In 1927 the Government of Northern Ireland set up a Committee to report on the situation of the Clogher Valley Tramway. The team of three had Robert Killin as the technical expert. A 37 page report was produced that recommended the line should focus on the carriage of freight and advocated the purchase of an Atkinson-Walker steam tractor. It entered service in 1929 on trial, but it was soon realised that the engine was underpowered and too slow. It was returned to the manufacturers for modifications, but they proved ineffective and it went back to Atkinson-Walker, who went into liquidation. The tractor failed to be sold and it went into storage. In 1931 the Donegal Railway expressed an interest and purchased it. The idea was to remove all the steam equipment and power it with a Gardner diesel engine. This was done and it entered service on freight and shunting duties. Given the name 'Phoenix' and numbered 11, it ran until the end of the railway and can now be seen in the Ulster Folk and Transport Museum.

The next railcar was number 12 which was an articulated bogie unit with a Walker diesel engine and a body and chassis built at the Dundalk works. It entered service in 1934 and set the pattern for all future railcars on the Donegal line. It was the largest railcar the Donegal had purchased up to that date, with seating for 41 passengers. It continued to give service until the line closed. Today it is at the Foyle Valley Railway.

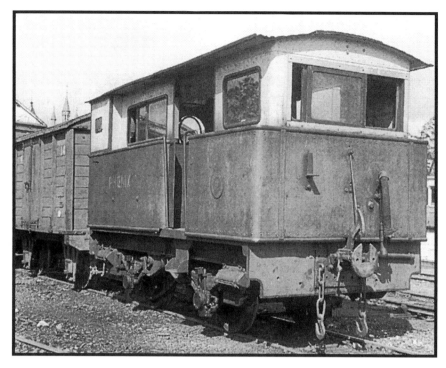

The ex-Clogher Valley Tramway had a steam tractor that was a failure. It was returned to its manufacturer and eventually sold to the County Donegal Railway who converted it to diesel power.

In 1934 the two railcars, numbers 2 and 3, from the Derwent Valley Railway were no longer fit for service. They were replaced by two second hand cars. When the Castlederg and Victoria Bridge Tramway closed the Donegal line purchased the chassis of their railcar. A new petrol engine and 32 seat body were fitted and the car entered service. It was given the number 2. The other replacement car was purchased second-hand from the Dublin and Blessington tramway. This was a Drewry petrol bogie car that was unique on the Donegal in having driving positions at both ends. It ran as a railcar until 1943 when it was converted into a trailer.

In 1935 two more Walker articulated powered railcars, numbers 14 and 15, were purchased. They each had a seating capacity of 41 passengers. In the following year a similar railcar, number 16 was added to the fleet. 1938 and 1939 saw the addition of numbers 17 and 18, each with seats for 43 passengers. Number 18 is now on the Fintown Railway. Another second hand railcar came to the line in 1942, this time from the Clogher Valley. This was another Walker powered articulated diesel unit with 28 seats. Following the closure of the line this railcar became an exhibit at the Ulster Folk and Transport Museum, where it can still be seen. The final two railcars had Walker diesel engines and were supplied in 1950 and 1951 respectively. After the closing of the line in 1961 they were both sold to the Isle of Man Railways where they worked for many years. In 1998 they were withdrawn for restoration.

Although the County Donegal line closed in 1960 it is possible to ride on part of the line on the Fintown Railway. Railcar number 18, hauled by a Simplex 102T diesel locomotive, carries passengers on the 1½ mile long line that runs alongside the shores of Loch Finn.

The second number 3 came from the Dublin and Blessington tramway when it closed. It was a Drewry petrol bogie car that was unique on the Donegal Railway railcars in having driving positions at both ends.

County Donegal Railway railcar number 18 survives and here is pictured being hauled on the Fintown Heritage Railway.

COUNTY DONEGAL RAILWAYS JOINT COMMITTEE PETROL AND DIESEL RAILCARS

Date Entered Service	Fleet No	Type	Manufacturer	Date Ceased Service	Notes
1906	1	Service car	Allday & Onions	1956	Rebuilt as a passenger railcar in 1920
1926	2	Railcar	Ford	1956	Ex-Derwent Valley Railway
1926	3	Railcar	Ford	1956	Ex-Derwent Valley Railway
1928	4	Railcar	Dundalk Works	1947	
1929	5	Railcar	Dundalk Works	1946	
1930	6	Railcar	Dundalk Works		Converted to trailer in 1945
1931	7	Railcar	Dundalk Works	1949	First diesel railcar in Britain
1931	8	Railcar	Dundalk Works	1949	First diesel railcar in Britain
1933	9	Railcar	Converted bus	1949	
1933	10	Railcar	Converted bus	1940	Destroyed by fire
1933	11	Shunter	Converted from steam	1960	Ex-Clogher Valley Tramway, 'Phoenix' now in the Ulster Folk and Transport Museum
1934	12	Railcar	Dundalk Works	1960	Now on the Foyle Valley Railway
1934	2	Railcar	CVBT	1960	Ex-Castleberg and Victoria Bridge Tramway
1934	3	Railcar	Drewry	1960	Converted to trailer in 1943
1935	14	Railcar	Walker Bros	1960	
1935	15	Railcar	Walker Bros	1960	
1936	16	Railcar	Walker Bros	1960	
1938	17	Railcar	Walker Bros	1960	
1939	18	Railcar	Walker Bros	1960	Now on the Fintown Heritage Railway
1942	10	Railcar	Walker Bros	1960	
1950	19	Railcar	Walker Bros	1960	Sold to Isle of Man Railways
1951	20	Railcar	Walker Bros	1960	Sold to Isle of Man Railways

MOTOR RAIL AND TRAM CAR COMPANY LIMITED (SIMPLEX), 1909

The story of these tramcars starts in India where J. D. Abbott (Resident Executive Engineer of the East India Tramways Company) wanted to mechanise the Karachi horse tramway. The normal choice of electricity was prohibitively expensive and so he considered petrol power. He had patented a gearbox ideal for tramcars that had two speeds in either direction. A four feet gauge sample car was built at the Phoenix Ironworks, in Lewes, in 1909 and sent to Karachi. It proved a success and the Chairman of the Tramway Company (who happened to be the father of Mr Abbott) suggested forming a Company to acquire the patent and use it to make further tramcars. The Motor Rail and Tram Car Company Limited was established in 1911. The Chairman, Secretary and address of the new Company were the same as for the Karachi Tramway. The first move was to acquire the patent for the gearbox, which became known as the Simplex gearbox.

In 1911 the first order was for 30 petrol tramcars that were built in Lewes at the Phoenix Ironworks and shipped out to the East India Tramway in Karachi. There was an order for one tramcar from the Siamese State Railway later that year, however, before it could be fulfilled the order was cancelled. In December 1912 there was an order for 10 tramcar chassis from the Baroda Tramway, India. But, after some of the chassis were delivered, the tramway reneged on their payment and no further tram chassis were delivered. In 1914 there was an order for two petrol tram chassis from the Lombardy Road-Rail Company for a tramway in the Lombardy district of Northern Italy. The bodies of the tramcars were to be made locally in Italy. In 1915 an order came from the State of Bhavnagar railway in India. A single vehicle was ordered and was referred to as a petrol railcar, but it was effectively a crossbench tramcar. The whole vehicle was constructed in Lewes.

An early petrol tramcar built by the Motor Rail and Tram Car Company Limited for the East India Tramway Company in Karachi.

In the lead up to the World War 1 the Directors realised that a light petrol locomotive could be used to support military action. Once war started the War Department ordered a variety of locomotives including the very light Simplex produced by Motor Rail. It proved extremely practical and large numbers were ordered. Production moved to Bedford and altogether around 1,000 such locomotives were manufactured, leaving no time for any other products. The end of the war, in 1918, brought an end to these orders. In 1919 the East India Tramway ordered 10 semi-closed petrol trams, with a corridor along the centre of the tram, giving greater protection to passengers in the rainy season and were made in the Bedford factory. A further ten were ordered in 1921.

From 1914 the Company made a number of larger bogie railcars that were far more allied to railway stock and outside the remit of this book. However, in 1921 the Western Australian Government Railways contacted the Motor Rail Company to order three tramcar chassis for use on rural branch lines that were lightly laid. Each vehicle had a 40 seat capacity and although seen as tramcar chassis in the factory, they were referred to as railcars by the railway. The bodies were constructed locally in Australia. The Siamese State Railway contacted the Company in 1922 to order three tramcar chassis, an order that was honoured on this occasion! Clearly the railway was very satisfied with the vehicles as they ordered a further six tramcars and an equal number of trailers in 1923. The chassis were shipped to Siam and the tramcar bodies were added locally.

A later, more enclosed, version of the petrol tramcar for Karachi.

After WW1 the Company made four-wheel passenger rail vehicles that closely resembled the tramcars, but were ordered as inspection railcars for a variety of railways, including the military. Other customers included the Midland Railway in England, the Darjeeling-Himalayan Railway in India, the Victoria Railway in West Nigeria and a small railcar for China. In addition there were orders for a variety of narrow gauge industrial petrol locomotives and wagons, again outside the scope of this volume.

The East India Tramway in Karachi was a regular customer of the Motor Rail Company. The records are not clear, but it would appear that between 1921 and 1947 around 70 tramcar chassis were produced and sold to the tramway Company. They ran until the Karachi Tramways closed in 1975. As the demand for light locomotives increased there were less orders for tramcars and demand had virtually ceased by 1931. The Company decided to change its name from the Motor Rail and Tram Car Company Limited to Motor Rail Limited. The name was changed again in 1972 to Simplex Mechanical Handling Limited (the Company had been using Simplex as a trading name since its creation). In 1987 the locomotive side of the Company was sold to Alan Keefe Limited, Ross on Wye, who has continued to build some locomotives and provide spares.

IMPERIAL INTERNATIONAL EXHIBITION, WHITE CITY, LONDON 1909

The Imperial International Exhibition was held at the White City in 1909. Opened by the Duke of Argyll on 20th May it lasted for five months. It followed the Franco-British Exhibition that had been held the previous year and the Imperial International Exhibition used many of the earlier exhibits, but with many additional attractions, making it a larger event. To assist visitors around the large site, a tramway line was built and the Sidney Straker and Squire Limited Company took the opportunity to present their newly introduced petrol tramcars.

Twelve tramcars were supplied, all to the same design, with a petrol-mechanical power source, and the bodies built by the United Electric Company, Preston. This simple tramway also illustrated some of the complexities surrounding tramway promoters. There was confusion as to the appropriate Authority to issue the necessary licence. Fairground type rides at the Exhibition came under the auspices of the London County Council. However, it was determined that this was a tramway and needed a licence from the Metropolitan Police. They inspected the line and agreed to it, provided the speed was limited to eight miles per hour. The petrol engine was a 32 b.h.p.

four cylinder unit made by Straker-Squire. The drive was the mechanical type with a clutch and a gearbox with two forward speeds and one reverse. The driving position was at one end only and the tramway required turntables at the termini. Unusually for tramcars (but possibly influenced by the bus background of the manufacturer) the speed was controlled by an accelerator pedal although the brakes were the more normal tramcar hand operated screw on type. Rather oddly the tramcars had three axles, with a bogie at one end of the car while at the other there was a single driven axle. The body used a cross bench design that allowed passengers a full view over the Exhibition site as they completed their journey.

One of the White City tramcars on a turntable at the terminus of the route.

There is no record of the subsequent history of these tramcars. However, in 1911 an order was placed for two similar vehicles by the Curaçaoschen Tramwegdienst Company of Willemstad (capital of the island of Curaçao in the Southern Caribbean Sea). The bodies were built by the United Electric Company, Preston and the mechanical equipment by Straker Squire. These tramcars were able to be driven from both ends and were slightly larger than the White City cars. The initial move by Straker Squire to build the petrol tramcars may have been influenced by an order placed in 1908 by João Pessoa, a town in Brazil, for two petrol tramcars. These were built by the United Electric Company with mechanical equipment from Leyland.

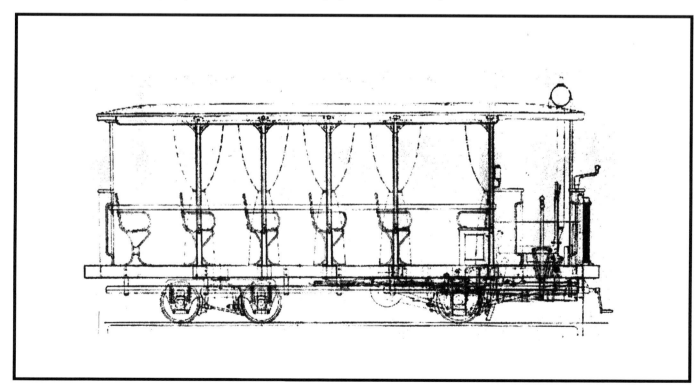

A drawing of the Straker-Squire petrol tramcar design used at the Imperial International Exhibition held at the White City in 1909. Note the three axle chassis, single ended driving position and cross-bench seating.

MORECAMBE PETROL TRAMS 1912 - 1924

A horse drawn tramway was opened in Morecambe in 1887 by the Morecambe Tramways Company. In the early 1900s the Corporation was interested in acquiring the tramway and reached an agreement with the tramway Company to purchase it. However, the public of Morecambe were not convinced, believing it would run at a loss and be a drain on the rates. At a public meeting in 1908 the Councillors were shouted down. Disregarding the public view, the Corporation obtained authority from Parliament in 1909 to operate the tramway. Once they owned the line the Corporation set about doubling the track over long sections of the line from East View to Battery Hotel (the Morecambe Tramway still owned the line from the Battery Hotel to Strawberry Gardens that had been built later and was not yet able to be purchased compulsorily). The Corporation was under pressure to electrify the line, as it would be less expensive to run. They chose to continue running with horse tramcars, possibly there was objection to spoiling the sea front with overhead wires as the Corporation considered using battery operated tramcars. However, the Corporation line only ever operated with horse tramcars, finally closing on 6th October 1926.

Morecambe petrol tramcar number 1, the postcard suggests that this was taken on the opening of the petrol tram service.

The section of line not under Corporation operation, from the Battery Hotel to Strawberry Gardens, continued to be operated by the Morecambe Tramway Company. Now they had 1¼ miles of route and just three horse trams (all the others had gone to the Corporation) and an obligation to provide a service for the whole year. The Company had one other thing, a pocket full of cash from the sale of the rest of the line. It was time for it to purchase some more tramcars. The natural move would have been to convert the tramway to electric operation. However, it is likely that they knew that the Corporation was averse to overhead electric wire and the capital expense of electricity generating plant and costly overhead equipment would have been disproportionate to the small size of the tramway. For around nine months of the year the population, including holiday makers, was around 15,000, but for the remainder of the year there were just 3,000 residents. Battery operation was examined but in 1911 the Company chose to order three petrol trams from Leyland Motors Limited, better known for making omnibuses. The tramcars were ordered and delivered in 1912, becoming the first petrol tramcars to operate a public street tramway service in Great Britain.

During the First World War petrol became scarce and Morecambe tramways fitted the three enclosed petrol tramcars with roof mounted gas bags so that the cars could run on town gas.

The trams were single deck, enclosed, open vestibule cars with 55 hp petrol engines and carrying 37 passengers. There was a driving platform on each end of the car, each of which had a complete set of driving controls. The standard Leyland engine was located on one of the platforms with a drive shaft going under the saloon to power the axle furthest from the engine. The chassis had an 8ft. long wheelbase with driving wheels of 30in. diameter. There was a four speed gear box giving speeds of 3.3, 6, 9 and 12mph. A gear enabled the drive to be reversed giving an equal range of speeds in either direction. The axles were linked with a heavy chain giving a four-wheel drive. There were two types of brake, the usual tramway type handbrake and unusually for trams, a foot operated brake acting on a drum mounted band brake on the drive shaft. The car body was supplied by the United Electric Car Company Limited, Preston. It was roomy and well-finished, and had side windows which could be raised and lowered by screw operating gear. The car was illuminated by a number of 10 candle-power 6-volt electric metallic filament lamps, supplied with current from a dynamo driven from the engine on the Trier and Martin system.

The general dimensions of the vehicle were: length over collision fenders, 31ft. width overall 7ft. 7in; length over corner pillars, 21ft. 6in; total height, 10ft. 1½in; gauge, 4ft 8in; wheel base, 8ft; weight of car complete, 7 tons 5 cwt. It appears that these were a success as the Company realised in 1913 that a greater carrying capacity was needed for the summer months and placed an order for a fourth tramcar, but this time without windows or a roof, rather like the 'Boat' trams in Blackpool, but four-wheel not bogie. Otherwise the rest of the tramcar, including all the mechanical elements, was the same as the first three. The trams gave good service and were more economical to run than the horse trams. However, the First World War brought new problems, with a shortage of petrol. Indeed, many petrol buses were being converted to run on town gas by fitting gas bags to the roof. The Morecambe Tramway Company decided to do the same and a wooden framework was fitted to the roof to hold the large gas bag. The open tramcar was unsuitable to convert as there was no roof on which to mount the gas bag, limiting the service to three cars.

The gas container on each car had a capacity of nearly 900 cu. ft. The containers were manufactured by Messrs John Knape and Sons, Burnley, and were said to be among the largest gas containers in existence. At the end of the War the three enclosed tramcars were changed back to petrol. However, following the end of the war bus competition increased and in Heysham the flexibility of buses enabled them to penetrate to the centre of the town. The tiny tramway was unable to compete and it closed on 24th October 1924, though few noticed. The trams were sold to a local ship breaker and were scrapped. Thus ended the country's first petrol powered tramcars.

LEYLAND MOTOR LIMITED, JOHANNESBURG TRAMWAYS 1912

When Leyland Motor Limited manufactured the four petrol tramcars for Morecambe they sold six of the same design of enclosed car to Johannesburg. These were made by the factory in Leyland, Lancashire. Shipped out to Johannesburg very little is known of the history of these tramcars or why they were ordered by a system that was already using electric power for its tramway.

LONDON COUNTY COUNCIL PETROL TRAMS 1913 - 1922

In the 1890s the London County Council decided to take over the horse tramways in their area with the intention of electrifying the whole system. Having regard of the cost to rate payers the Council chose to wait the 21 years defined in the Tramways Acts enabling them to take over the tramways at the 'scrap' price and not at the price of a going concern. As the horse tramways had been built at various times, the acquisitions were spread over many years. One route was the horse tramway that ran between South Hackney and West India Docks (route 71). This was a relatively lightly used service and the LCC was loath to commit the capital expenditure of installing the conduit system of current supply. The route went through three local boroughs, Hackney, Bethnal Green and Stepney and they were adamant that they would not allow overhead electric wires to be erected over the streets. The LCC had previously experimented with stud contact along the Mile End Road. It had been a conspicuous failure and the LCC were not going to try that approach again. They were aware that omnibuses were being developed with petrol -electric systems. This seemed to be a solution to the problem. The Board of Trade was approached and they agreed that the LCC could use petrol-electric tramcars without need for new legislation, however, some changes were required to the position of the tracks to meet their safety requirements.

One of the three petrol tramcars owned by the London County Council. The trams were easily identifiable by the mesh covered hole in the dash panel allowing air to circulate over the radiator and the conspicuous noise the vehicle made travelling along the street.

Few people have ever witnessed the driver of a tramcar having to use a starting handle on the motor to get the car going. No doubt the driver was embarrassed by this publicity shot for the tramway.

In 1912 three redundant horse tramcars were taken and petrol-electric equipment ordered from W. A. Stevens at Maidstone, Kent, who were the suppliers of this type of power unit for omnibuses. The tramcars were numbered P1, P2 and P3. The cars were taken to Charlton Depot where the platforms and canopies were extended, higher decency panels were installed around the upper deck with 90° direct staircases. The petrol engine was 40 h.p. mounted on one of the platforms, under the stairs, and it drove an electric generator. On the other platform, also under the stairs, was the radiator, with a large round grill cut in the side of the dash panel. To cool the generator, it was fitted with an electrically powered fan. There was an electric motor fitted to each axle, that provided the drive. These were driven from either end of the car through a normal tram controller.

The first trials with two of the tramcars began on 7th May 1913, using route 70 from Greenwich to London Bridge. They were not a success. The LCC found that they were very expensive to run and the passengers complained of the noise and noxious fumes. The trials ceased on 9th December 1913 and the three tramcars were placed in storage. They were taken out of storage in December 1914 and the bodies removed and low sides fitted to make an open wagon. They were sent to the trailer depot at Marius Road, Balham. Here they were used as tractors to shunt the trailer cars in and out of the depot. Use of trailers ceased in November 1922 and there was no use for the tractors, so they were scrapped.

In addition to these petrol tramcars the LCC and then London Transport had a vast fleet of ancillary support vehicles, both petrol and diesel. These were allocated to the tramways, the trolleybuses and the buses. There was a degree of interchangeability between the three parts of the organisation. The focus of this book is on those vehicles that had a primary role supporting the tramway service. Over the years there were a total of sixteen dedicated petrol breakdown lorries that would take engineers to disabled tramcars where roadside repairs would be effected, or to keep the service running, to tow or push the tramcars back to the nearest depot. This was a particular need for London as the conduit system was prone to damage. In the central area, the tramcars received electricity through ploughs mounted under the tramcars. If the plough become jammed it would be ripped from its mounting, cutting power from the car. Also a track brake would sometimes be broken and it ended damaging the plough carrier with the same effect. The emergency crew would cut the plough off the car using an acetylene torch, allowing the lower part to drop into the conduit. The tramcar would then be pushed back to the nearest depot.

There were also three petrol conduit cleaners, which were water carriers that operated rather like gulley cleaners. Finally, there was a tractor with solid rubber tyres. This was based at the Charlton Central Repair Depot (along with others) and was used to manoeuvre tramcars around the depot, as the depot had no overhead or conduit supply. It appears that number 351X (registration number CUC 192) was primarily used for this duty, though during the scrapping of tramcars in 1952 it was assisted by other tractors. They were fitted with large rubber or matting surfaced buffers front and rear so that they could push trams, trolleybuses and buses as required. They also had hooks to enable a chain to be attached for towing. Many of the tramway ancillary vehicles lasted to the end of the tramways and some continued to work servicing the trolleybus fleet. One of the Fordson tractors has been preserved and is on display at the East Anglia Transport Museum, Carlton Colville. Number 626X, it was one of the vehicles that was not registered. If it needed to travel on the public highway it was fitted with trade plates. There is a second ancillary support Fordson tractor that has also been preserved. Number 351X (registration number CUC 192), it is currently in private ownership.

Petrol tractor number 626X at the East Anglia Transport Museum.

As can be seen the petrol engine is a standard motor car engine and was fitted onto one of the tramcar's platforms. The exhaust was led under the vehicle away from passengers and pedestrians.

A breakdown lorry pushes a disabled tramcar and it looks like it is about to take on
another tramcar. There is no sign of any repair work, suggesting that this section of track
has lost all power and the lorry is retrieving both of them pending repairs to the power supply.

Creating a great deal of interest for the spectators, a petrol tractor pushes a tramcar
into the scrap yard to await its breaking up. This was the fate of all but a
few tramcars when the London tramway ceased running.

Looking very clean and new, three tramway breakdown tenders are lined up outside a tram depot for this publicity photograph. The most frequent causes for a call out were problems with the plough and conduit. A flame cutter was carried to cut off the plough in order to free the tramcar to be towed away.

London County Council petrol car number P1 undergoing trials in the street. The damp day does nothing to raise spirits, particularly as the tramcars proved unsuitable for the job they were designed for.

LONDON COUNTY COUNCIL AND LONDON TRANSPORT TRAMWAY ANCILLARY FLEET

Date in Service	No	Reg	Description	Colour	Date Scrapped
1919	72Z	LH8442	AEC Tyler 5-ton Towing Lorry	Grey	1940
1920	136	XB9002	British Ensign 6-ton Tramway Breakdown Tender		1937
1929	173K	UW1264	Karrier 6-ton Tramway Breakdown Tender with Crane	Red	1952
1929	174K	UW1265	Karrier 6-ton Tramway Breakdown Tender with Crane	Red	1952
1930	175K	GH9732	Karrier 6 1/4-ton Tramway Breakdown Tender with Crane	Red	1952
1930	176K	GH9733	Karrier 6 1/4-ton Tramway Breakdown Tender with Crane	Red	1952
1930	177K	GH9734	Karrier 6 1/4-ton Tramway Breakdown Tender with Crane	Red	1952
1930	178K	GH9735	Karrier 6 1/4-ton Tramway Breakdown Tender with Crane	Red	1949
1930	7	TP (Trade Plate)	Associated Daimler 418 2 1/2-ton Tramway Breakdown Lorry	?	1938
1930	9	TP	Associated Daimler 418 2 1/2-ton Tramway Breakdown Lorry	?	1938
1930	70	TP	Associated Daimler 418 2 1/2-ton Tramway Breakdown Lorry	?	1938
1930	81	TP	Associated Daimler 418 2 1/2-ton Tramway Breakdown Lorry	?	1938
1930	82	MY4614	Associated Daimler 418 2 1/2-ton Tramway Breakdown Lorry	?	1939
1931	124	HX38	Ford Ensign 30-cwt Tramway Breakdown Tender	?	1937
By 1934		TP	British Ensign 6-tom Tramway Breakdown Van	?	1937
1934	179K	TP	Karrier 6 3/4-ton Tramway Breakdown Tender with Crane & Tower Unit	Red	1952
1937	351X	CUC192	Fordson 1 3/4-ton Tractor (Solid Tyres)	Green	1960
1938	113W	PG7681	AEC Regal 5 1/2-ton 1000-gallon Tramway Conduit Cleaner	Green	1953
1938	112W	PL6471	AEC Regal 5 1/2-ton 1000-gallon Tramway Conduit Cleaner	Green	1953
1948	742J	AUC596	AEC Regent 110HP 1000-gallon Tramway Conduit Cleaner	Green	1953

One of the tractors towing a Feltham tramcar at Charlton Central Repair Depot

STIRLING AND BRIDGE OF ALLAN 1913 - 1920

The Stirling and Bridge of Allan Tramway was a short, 3½ mile long, horse tramway that ran from Stirling to the community at the Bridge of Allan, opening in 1874. From 1878 the Company examined a number of ways to mechanise the tramway including steam tramway locomotives and erecting an electric overhead supply (that the authorities objected to). However, all these came to nought and horse trams continued to run on the line. In 1898 the line was extended a mile from King Street, Stirling to St Ninians. By the 1910s there were many comments about the antiquity of the horse tramcars. Thoughts turned again to electrifying the system, but again there were objections from the local authorities. The Tramway felt they needed to gain the benefits of mechanisation and so they decided to trial a petrol driven tram.

The ex-horse car number 22 that was converted into a petrol powered car. It became the only powered car in the Stirling fleet. It was scrapped when the tramway closed in 1920.

They experienced difficulty finding a Company that could build the car, finally finding the Lanarkshire Motor Company in Glasgow. Horse tramcar number 22 was sent to the works where a 25 hp Commer petrol engine was fitted on one of the platforms, protruding down to enable the prop shaft to drive a three speed gearbox that powered a central lay shaft that drove both axles through chain drives. A new chassis was built with a wheelbase 6in. longer than the original. Driving controls were fitted to both platforms. It was given trial runs in Glasgow before being sent to Stirling. In Stirling it was usually used on the short St Ninians route as it had a steep section that needed a trace horse. The car proved to be very successful and it was used every day except Sundays, when no trams ran, this day was used to carry out maintenance. Further attempts were made to interest commercial companies to buy the tramway and convert it to electric operation. The Council considered purchasing the system, but decided not to. Then Balfour Beatty was approached but that came to nought. The tramway continued running with horse trams and the single petrol tramcar. Finally, the tramway was sold to the Scottish General Omnibus Company Limited and the tramway ceased operations, being replaced by buses. For the last three months the horse trams ceased running, but the petrol tram was still in service. The petrol tram ceased running on 20th May 1920 with the complete closure of the tramway.

JOYCE GREEN HOSPITAL, DARTFORD 1914/1921 - 1936

Joyce Green Hospital was opened in 1903 as an isolation hospital for smallpox victims. It was to replace three hospital ships moored on the Thames. It became part of the Dartford Hospitals complex, a large area with several hospitals, all handling contagious illnesses. To provide a transport system, a horse tramway was built within the grounds. In 1914 the hospital authorities experimented with petrol ambulances hauling the tramcars. However, the war meant a shortage of petrol and the horses continued to be the source of power. Then in 1922 the idea was resurrected and another trial was undertaken with petrol as the source of power. This was welcomed as a success and regular use of motor ambulances was introduced in May 1925, although it looked a little odd for an ambulance with rubber tyres to be hauling a steel wheeled tram trailer along a railed track. The use of ambulance power continued until 1936, by which time patients were being brought into the hospital grounds by motor ambulances that were able to drive directly to the wards. The tramway was closed and the rails lifted in 1943 as part of the scrap metal war-time initiative. The ambulances went back to their more normal activities.

Two of the Joyce Green ambulances being hauled by the motor ambulance through the grounds.

HASTINGS PETROL TRAMS 1914 - 1921

The Hastings and District Electric Tramways Company commenced operating electric tramways in July 1905 with two separate sections, one in Hastings town and the other from St Leonards to Bexhill. The connection between the towns was along the promenade and the Hastings Council would not give permission for overhead electric wires to be erected along their beautiful seafront. There was also severe opposition from property owners along the promenade. When the tramway first opened there was no agreement about what type of power supply could be used. The Councils agreed to a stud contact system along the seafront and the two parts of the tramway were joined when that section of line opened in 1907. However, as is now well known, stud contact had many difficulties. In addition to much sparking the studs would often stay live after the car had passed. A wire brush fitted to the fender of the car would contact the stud and if it was live a bell would ring on the platform. This was the signal for the conductor to grab a wooden mallet and give the offending stud a sharp tap to release the switch and turn the stud off. However, the stud length of line became more unreliable and subject to damage from sand and spray. The tramway Company decided on another solution.

They had clearly heard about the petrol-electric tramcars and chose this answer to the problem. It is thought all the twenty tramcars that were fitted for the stud system were all modified to operate as petrol-electric tramcars, with a petrol engine and generator purchased from W. A. Stevens in Maidstone. The tramcars had rather unusual driving controls. In addition to the usual electric controller on each platform, there was another, smaller, controller that regulated the electric from the generator to the car motors. The change took place in March 1914 and the petrol-electric tramcars continued to run until 1921. It was soon realised that the petrol engines were grossly

Tramcars on the promenade section of the Hastings tramways where the Council banned the use of overhead wires.

underpowered and crawled along the promenade. The Council finally gave in and allowed the overhead wire to be erected, with a full overhead electric operation starting in March 1921. The tramcars had the petrol engines and generators removed.

DUBLIN AND BLESSINGTON TRAMWAY 1915 – 1932

The Dublin and Blessington Tramway opened as a steam operated roadside tramway in August 1888. The 5ft. 3in. gauge tramway ran from Blessington to Terenure, South Dublin, some 15 miles long. There was a 3-mile line from Terenure to the centre of Dublin, but this was over Dublin United Tramways track. The Blessington line ran with double deck trailers hauled by steam tram locomotives. The line from Blessington was extended 4½ miles to Poullaphouca in 1895 by the Blessington and Poullaphouca Steam Tramway.

By 1911 the steam tram locomotives were wearing out. Serious consideration was given to electrifying the line to Crooksling and then using trailers with petrol-electric power units for the remaining 11½ miles to provide electricity to the tramcars. However, costings were not favourable and other events overtook the plans with the outbreak of WW1. In 1915 the Company decided to purchase two bogie petrol-electric tramcars. Numbered 1 and 2 the lower deck was totally enclosed but the upper deck was entirely open. The cars seated 26 in the lower saloon and 46 on the upper deck. The bodies were 33ft. long and they had vertical Aster petrol engines driving a 65 kw generator and the cars could be driven from either end. In operation the cars proved to be grossly underpowered, very complicated and unreliable. They proved so bad that they were soon withdrawn. The engines were taken back by the makers and the bogies were acquired by the Dublin United Tramway.

One of the two petrol-electric tramcars purchased by the Dublin and Blessington Tramway. They proved to be unsuccessful and were soon withdrawn and scrapped.

Dublin and Blessington Number 2, one of the two Ford railcars acquired in 1925. It is believed that the chassis were purchased from Ford, while the bodies were built by the railway Company.

The service continued with the steam tram locomotives until 1925, when two Ford Model T petrol chassis were acquired. It is believed that the tramway built the bodies using what remained from the two failed petrol-electric tramcars. The outcome was a pair of four-wheel railcars with single deck bodies seating 16 passengers. The limited capacity meant that they were used during light traffic demand, reducing running costs. One slight difficulty was that they were single ended and so required turning facilities at their termini. Small turntables were fitted at Blessington, Jobstown, Tallaght and Terenure. A year later a third petrol driven railcar, number 3, was purchased, this time from the Drewry Car Company. It was a single deck 40 seating bogie car with maximum traction bogies each having the larger diameter wheels driven. In order to accommodate the petrol engines there were holes in the passenger compartment floors. To protect the passengers, the engines were boxed in, forcing passengers to sidle past. It had driving controls at both ends and so did not require turntables.

Already losing money, the tramway lost more revenue when a local bus service was established in 1929, followed soon by another bus company. The tramway decided to cease operations at the end of 1932. The physical assets of the Company were advertised for sale. One of the Ford petrol railcoaches and the Drewry car were sold to County Donegal Railways where they were regauged to 3ft. The Drewry car was used until 1943 when it was converted to a trailer car by removing the motors. It continued in service and when County Donegal Railways closed it was acquired by the Ulster Folk and Transport Museum, Cultra, where it is on display.

Dublin and Blessington purchased a Drewry railcar in 1926. It was unusual in having maximum traction bogies, clearly shown in this photograph

CONCLUSIONS

The use of petrol engines in tramcars was close to becoming more accepted in Britain when the LCC tried three out in 1913. Unfortunately, they proved such a failure that they never entered the service they were intended for, but were withdrawn and ended up as works cars. Hastings had an unfortunate experience with stud contact and had a similar time with petrol power, finally being able to persuade the local Council to accept overhead wires along the seafront. The most successful use of petrol power was at Joyce Green Hospital where motor ambulances pulled horse trams. As the ambulances were both available and proven it is not surprising that they were a success. However, all this was on private land and it is uncertain whether the Board of Trade were asked for permission or even knew about their use. It is highly unlikely that there would have been authorisation to use them on the public highway with other road traffic.

FURTHER READING

SCOTTISH MOTOR ENGINEERING COMPANY LIMITED
Trams Without Wires—Postscript: by Alan W. Brotchie and David H. Bayes, Scottish Transport No 42 December 1987.

MOTOR RAIL COMPANY
A Guide to Simplex Narrow Gauge Locomotives: by D. R. Hall and J. A. Rowlands, pub. The Mosely Railway Trust, 2001.
The Early Years of the Motor Rail and Tram Car Company 1911 – 1931: by W. J. K. Davies, pub. Plateway Press 2008.
Motor Rail Ltd: by Alan M. Keef, pub. Lightmoor Press, 2016.

IMPERIAL INTERNATIONAL EXHIBITION, WHITE CITY, LONDON 1909
Commercial Motor: 27th May 1909, 8th July 1909

MORECAMBE PETROL TRAMS
The Engineer 19th January 1912: page 78, Morecambe Petrol Tramcar.
Commercial Motor: 29th August 1918.
The Lancaster and Morecambe Tramways: by S. Shuttleworth, Locomotion Papers 99, pub. The Oakwood Press, 1976.
The Tramways of North Lancashire: by W. H. Bett and J. C. Gillham edited by J. H. Price, pub. Light Rail Transit Association, 1984.
Scottish Transport No 42 December 1986, Trams Without Wires: by Brian S. Skillen.

JOHANNESBURG TRAMWAYS
Scottish Transport No 42 December 1986, Trams Without Wires: by Brian S. Skillen.

LONDON COUNTY COUNCIL PETROL TRAMS
The Engineer 13th May 1913: page 587, Petrol-Electric Tramcar for the London County Council.
London County Council Tramways Handbook 3rd Edition: by Kennington, pub. Tramway and Light Railway Society, 1977.
Scottish Transport No 42 December 1986, Trams Without Wires: by Brian S. Skillen.
London County Council Tramways Vol 1 South London: by E. R. Oakley pub. London Tramways Historical Group, Tramway and Light Railway Society and Light Rail Transit Association, 1989.
LCC Electric Tramways: by Robert J. Harley, pub. Capital Transport 2002.

STIRLING AND BRIDGE OF ALLAN
The Tramways of Stirling: by Alan W. Brotchie, pub. The N.B. Traction Group, 1976
Scottish Transport No 42 December 1986, Trams Without Wires: by Brian S. Skillen.
Stirling's Trams and Buses: by A. W. Brotchie, pub. N.B. Traction, 1991
The Tramways of Eastern Scotland: by J. C. Gillham and R. J. Wiseman, pub. Light Rail Transit Association, 2000.

JOYCE GREEN HOSPITAL, DARTFORD
The Tramways of Woolwich and South East London: by Southeastern pub. Light Railway Transport League and Tramway and Light Railway Society, 1963.
North Kent Tramways: by Robert J. Harley, pub. Middleton Press, 1994.

HASTINGS PETROL TRAMS
The Hastings Tramways Company, Paper presented to the National Trolleybus Association: 16th January 1974; by Lyndon W. Rowe 1974.
Tramway Review No 93 Spring 1978: letter from L. Heath.
Scottish Transport No 42 December 1986, Trams Without Wires: by Brian S. Skillen.
The Tramway of the South Coast: by J. C. Gillham and R. J. S. Wiseman, pub. Light Rail Transit Association, 2004.
Hastings Tramways: by Robert Harley, pub. Middleton Press, 1993.

DUBLIN AND BLESSINGTON TRAMWAY

The Narrow Gauge Railways of Ireland: by H. Fayle, published by Greenlake Publications Ltd., 1946
Irish Trams: by James Kilroy, published by Colourpoint, 1996

CHAPTER 4

MORE PETROL AND DIESEL TRAMS

MCEWAN PRATT AND COMPANY 1920

The McEwan Pratt and Company was a Company that manufactured locomotives with petrol/ paraffin engines for the overseas market. In 1920 they had an order for four petrol tramcars for the Nashik tramway in India. The tramway had been constructed in 1889 as a 5½ miles, 2ft. 6in. gauge, line connecting Nashik railway station with the centre of Nashik town. The system originally had two horse drawn tramcars and the line ran through dense jungle. In 1920 the horse drawn cars were replaced by four petrol-mechanical tramcars that had 45 hp petrol engines with a two speed gearbox directly driving one axle. The engine drove lay shafts, one for each direction of travel, each to its own final chain drive to a single axle. They continued to run until the tramway closed in the early 1930s.

KENT AND EAST SUSSEX RAILWAY 1920—1939

Col. Stephens was constantly seeking ways to reduce the running costs of his railways. To this end he experimented with using petrol power to replace the steam locomotives. By the end of WW1 the internal combustion petrol engine had developed into the preferred power source for road vehicles and Col. Stephens felt that this could be a way forward. In this he was a world pioneer as only one or two such experiments had been tried. He chose a car chassis from a second hand Wolseley-Siddeley car, disabled the steering, fitted metal flanged wheels to run on rails and built a lorry body. Around 1920 he tested on the Kent and East Sussex Railway. The trials must have been encouraging as he soon fitted an 18 seat saloon in place of the lorry body and it entered service. It ran on the Kent and East Sussex Railway for around four years before being moved to the Selsey Tramway in 1924.

The initial Ford railmotor set that entered service in 1923.

The savings must have been immediately apparent as in 1922 Col. Stephens purchased two 1 ton Ford chassis from Edmonds Motors and had 20 seat saloons fitted by Eaton Coachworks. He had realised that one disadvantage of the single railcar was that it was awkward for the driver to travel in reverse, as the large passenger body obscured the view backwards. He resolved this by ordering two vehicles and connecting them back to back. The vehicle facing the direction of travel provided the power, while the other would have its engine stopped and the gearbox placed in neutral. The pair entered passenger service on 15th February 1923. After some initial mechanical problems the pair settled into service.

Another pair of Ford railmotors was purchased from the same sources as the first and entered service in 1924. The two pairs of railmotors then took over many of the duties of the steam locomotives. They proved their worth in 1926 when the national coal strike restricted the use of coal, while petrol was still readily available. Unfortunately, the internal combustion engine did not have the long life of steam engines. By 1931 the first set succumbed to wear and it was withdrawn from use and the bodies were offered for sale in 1932. One railcar was sold for £1 10s and the other for a meagre 10s. The second set lasted another five years, finally being withdrawn from service in 1937 and the bodies sold in 1939.

The final railmotor set was made by Shefflex Lorries in 1930. The set was equipped with couplings at the ends allowing it to haul goods wagons (here an open truck).

To replace the previous railmotors a pair was ordered from Shefflex Lorries in 1930. They ran until being withdrawn in 1938 (and scrapped in 1941).

The line became under Government control in 1939 as part of the war arrangements. In 1948 it became part of the Southern Region of British Railways. Passenger services ceased in 1954, leaving just freight operation. The line finally closed in 1970. A preservation group was formed and they sought to open the line as a heritage steam railway. This took four years and the heritage service opened along part of the line in 1974. Surprisingly, the history of the line continues in this book as in 2017 a replica petrol railmotor arrived at Tenterden Station and is displayed outside the Col. Stephens Museum.

SHROPSHIRE AND MONTGOMERYSHIRE RAILWAY 1923—1937

The early history of the lines that were to become the Shropshire and Montgomeryshire is more convoluted than most railways. Thankfully the period where petrol power was used is very limited and we can pass rapidly over the beginnings. The Col. Stephens era begins in 1911 with the opening of the line under the Shropshire and Montgomeryshire name. The use of petrol did not start until 1923 when a railmotor set was purchased. The design of the motor cars was similar to the second set delivered to the Kent and East Sussex set, except that the Shropshire set had an unpowered passenger trailer that was connected between the two motor cars. The set was built by Edmonds Motors on a Ford chassis.

In operation the set ran as a two car set, the middle trailer being removed. It is believed that the reason for this was the lack of power of the powered cars combined with declining passenger numbers. Indeed the trailer coach was moved to the Selsey Tramway in 1930. The use of steam power diminished and there was more reliance on the railmotor that was more economic to run. No doubt in an attempt to reduce costs more the Selsey Tramway's Wolsey-Siddeley railmotor and petrol lorry were acquired in 1927, no doubt to the delight of the staff at Selsey, who disliked the pair. By 1930 the railmotors were becoming more unreliable and expensive to run. The Directors seriously considered scrapping them, but decided to carry on and they continued in service until 1936 though with a much reduced mileage. The regular passenger service had ended in 1933, but passenger specials continued to run. By this time the unusual steam locomotive 'Gazelle' had taken over the duties. The railmotor was parked on a siding and left to rot and it was demolished in 1941.

The Ministry of Defence took over running the remnants of the line in 1941 to service one of their ammunition depots. The railway probably ceased in 1959 when ammunition storage stopped and the rails were removed in 1961.

The three coach railmotor set made for the Shropshire and Montgomeryshire Railway. In reality the combination of lack of power and diminished passenger numbers meant that the centre unpowered coach was removed and the set operated as a two car unit.

SELSEY TRAMWAY 1924 – 1935

The Hundred of Manhood and Selsey Tramway was opened in 1897 as one of Col. Stephens light railways. It was built as a standard gauge light railway running from Chichester to Selsey. The original motive powers were small 0-4-2 and 0-6-0 tank engines. In the 1920s Col. Stephens was seeking to reduce the costs of his lines and he purchased a second hand Wolsey petrol motor car chassis. He fitted flanged wheels, a lorry body and tested it on the Kent and East Sussex Railway. It was later fitted with an 18 seat saloon and it ran in passenger service. In 1924 the railcar was transferred to the Selsey line (the name of which had changed to 'The West Sussex Railway', though it continued to be known as the Selsey Tramway). Initially operating as a single unit the railcar was driven in reverse for half its journeys. Later in the year it was joined by a modified Ford lorry. Coupled back to back the pair operated a passenger and goods service along the line until the Wolsey was damaged. Disliked by the staff the repairs took some time and when it was

The Ford lorry in its usual configuration with a flat wagon and back to back with the Wolsey railcar. The lorry was transferred to the Shropshire and Montgomeryshire Railway probably in 1927 soon after the Wolsey transfer. Photographs exist of them running as a pair in Shropshire.

in running order in 1927 it was transferred to the Shropshire and Montgomeryshire Railway. The Ford lorry stayed on the Selsey Tramway until being transferred to the Shropshire and Montgomeryshire Railway at an unknown later date, though probably not very long after the railcar.

The final petrol railcars that were purchased for the Selsey Tramway were this pair of Shefflex Motors railcars that arrived in 1928. Unusually they were owned by Col. Stephens rather than the tramway.

Col. Stephens approached the Ford Motor Company and ordered a purpose built three car railmotor set. This went to the Kent and East Sussex Railway. Following the resolving of some teething problems a two car set was ordered for the Selsey Tramway in 1924. This set ran back to back with a low sided open baggage truck between the two railcars. They lasted until the closure of the tramway in 1935. The final petrol railmotors to work on the Selsey Tramway were two 23 seat railmotors ordered from Shefflex Motors Ltd. in 1927 that were delivered the following year. Unusually these two were paid for not by the railway, but personally by Col. Stephens and remained his own property. Like the other units the two railmotors were connected back to back, often with a low sided open truck between them. The unit was scrapped soon after the line closed in 1935.

CASTLEDERG AND VICTORIA BRIDGE TRAMWAY 1925 - 1928

This line in County Tyrone, Northern Island ran to and from the two towns in its name. The 3ft. gauge tramway opened in 1883 with a stable of steam tank engines. The Board of Directors were always seeking ways to reduce costs and they heard that the County Donegal Railways had acquired a paraffin fuelled railcar (actually powered by petrol). They decided to acquire a similar car for their line and were going to approach the manufacturer of the Donegal car. However, the Locomotive Superintendent said that he and the workshop staff could build such a car. This was agreed and the construction of the 24 seat paraffin powered railcar was completed in 1925. However, the final cost was greater than the quotation from the outside manufacturer. It had a top speed of 30mph on the level with a fuel consumption of 8 to 10 miles per gallon.

The Castlederg railcar was unusual in being built by the tramway's workshop and using paraffin as its fuel.

In use the railcar could be driven from either end, though it had the appearance of a single ended vehicle, with a protruding bonnet at one end. Though it achieved the aim of saving running costs, it was noisier and more uncomfortable than the trains it replaced. It provided the service for three years and carried passengers for over 30,000 miles. It had an unusual three axle configuration, with two of the axles taking most of the weight, and an axle under the engine with smaller diameter wheels. In 1928 an inspection of the vehicle found it to be unfit for further use. It was parked in a siding and the following year the engine was removed and sold. The body deteriorated and was sold to the Donegal Railway. Here it was given a new engine and body. It ran in service for eleven years before being retired, donating parts for other cars. Then in 1944 it was rebuilt as a trailer where it continued service until 1959, when it was sold to become a summer house.

In 1929 a Kerr Stuart diesel locomotive was given trials on the tramway. However, it proved too weak for the work involved and it was returned to the manufacturer after just six months. In 1933 there was a strike of railway men over the whole of Northern Ireland causing the line to be closed by the Directors. The rolling stock and other assets were sold, mainly to scrap.

HERNE BAY PIER 1925 - 1935

The 3,613ft. long Herne Bay Pier was opened in 1832 with a hand-pushed luggage tramway. In the following year a wind powered sailing tram was used to carry both passengers and luggage. The tramway ceased when the pier closed due to storm damage in 1864. Repairs were delayed until 1872 with the pier reopening the following year. In 1898 it was lengthened by 74 ft. and by this time a 3ft. 4½in. gauge electric tramway had been laid. The tramway closed at the beginning of World War 1 and did not reopen until the end of the war when holiday makers returned to Herne Bay. A new tramway was opened in 1925 using a petrol-electric tramcar manufactured by the local company of Strode Engineering. The tramcar was unusual in having a centrally located petrol engine using a chain drive to power a generator that then provided electricity for the motors on the axles. It appears to have been both unreliable and underpowered and it became the butt

The nearer tramcar is the unsuccessful petrol electric tramcar that, by the time this photograph was taken, had been relegated to trailer duties, having had its power unit removed.

of jokes by the local people. The pier was proving more popular and a reliable tramcar was needed, but it was not until 1934 that a new tramcar arrived. The Pier Company had chosen a 48 seat battery powered tramcar from F. C. Hibbard and Company, built at their Park Royal Coach Works. However, it was not the end of the petrol-electric tramcar. The motors were all removed and it became a trailer for the new tram. They ran, carrying increasing numbers of passengers until the start of World War 2 when it ceased running again. The Herne Bay Pier was closed to the public for the security of the country, having been broken in two places. This saw the end of the tramway line.

RYE AND CAMBER TRAMWAY 1925 – 1939

The 3ft. gauge Rye and Camber Tramway was the first of Col Stephens' small light railways. Opened in 1895 it was built entirely on private land and so did not require Parliamentary permission. Indeed it was opened just 14 weeks after the creation of the Company. Being only on private land may be why Col Stephens chose to call it a tramway rather than a railway, though there is no specific reason why this was so. The purpose of the line was to take golfers from Rye station the less than two miles to Rye Golf Club. Initially a diminutive steam 2-4-0 tank locomotive, built by Bagnall, was the only motive power, hauling a single coach, also built by Bagnall and two open goods wagons (which were also used to carry passengers). The first locomotive, named 'Camber', was joined in 1897 by a similar Bagnall product, named 'Victoria' and a second coach built by the Rother Iron Works, Rye. In 1908 the line was extended from the Golf Club Station (renamed 'Golf Links') to Camber Sands to convey holiday makers. The two locomotives cont-

The diminutive Rye and Camber petrol locomotive at the rustic Camber Sands Station

inued to work the line until 1925. By this time use of the line had declined owing to automobile and bus competition. To reduce operating costs Col Stephens looked for less expensive motive power and in 1925 he purchased a diminutive 0-4-0 Simplex petrol tractor, built by the Kent Construction Company. This proved very successful and 'Victoria' was sold as scrap, while 'Camber' was kept as a reserve engine that was needed infrequently. However, the passing years saw the line decline and it became very run down. At the outbreak of World War 2 the passenger service ceased. It continued running under Government control to help in the construction of P.L.U.T.O. (the Pipe Line Under The Ocean). By the end of the war the line was in a very poor condition and it was decided not to re-open it, but rather sell it for scrap, which happened in 1947. The frame of one of the carriages exists at the Amberley Working Museum.

RYDE PIER TRAMWAY 1927 - 1969

The half mile long Ryde Pier opened in 1814, but was without any tramway until 1864 when a second pier was built alongside the first to give room for a tram line to be laid to link Ryde St John's Road Station with the ferries arriving at the pier. The first power source was a small steam locomotive. However, this proved rather too heavy as it set up dangerous vibrations on the pier. The pier owners stopped it running after just two trips and swiftly replaced it with horse tramcars. In 1877 a third pier was built to carry an extension of the Isle of Wight Railway from St John's Road Station to the end of the pier, thus eliminating the need for passengers to change conveyance. In 1881 there was another attempt to use steam tram locomotives. The problem this time was the dropping of hot embers and sparks onto the wooden pier threatening to set it alight.

Prudently the locomotives were withdrawn and the line returned to horse traction. The next source of power was electricity. The electrified tramway was opened in March 1889 with a converted double deck horse tram. New single deck cars were purchased from Pollards that hauled one or two of the old horse tramcars. The two tracks were run as independent single tracks. The pier was taken over by the Southern Railway in 1927, who decided to replace the aging electric units. In the same year the new Company purchased two Drewry petrol engine, single deck tramcars each with the capacity to carry 22 seated and 18 standing passengers. They had Baguley

26 h.p. petrol engines driving one axle through a four speed gearbox and chain drive. Unusually the trams could only be driven from one end (the landward end). Each tramcar hauled a single matching trailer. One of the trams sustained a damaged engine in 1933 and it was replaced with one from the local bus company until a proper replacement came from Drewry. In 1946 it was decided to replace the engines, as they had become worn out and two Bedford engines were ordered from Drewry. These lasted until 1959/60 when they too were replaced, this time with Perkins 30 hp diesel engines. During the fit, the gearboxes were replaced with four speed examples and the chain drives renewed. They continued in this condition until the pier tramway was closed on 26th January 1969, as it was no longer deemed safe to operate. The railway alongside continued in operation and is still used today.

One of the petrol railcars (with its trailer in front of it). It was common for the pair to have the flat wagon to carry luggage and goods.

The petrol trams were left abandoned by the pier entrance. Car number 2 was purchased by the Wight Locomotive Society. The chassis, engine and running gear were moved to Newport. Although the body had been removed the remainder was still operational and the Society used it as a works shunter, moving rolling stock around, particularly when they moved to Havenstreet. The Society was focussed on restoring railway items and the tram was set to one side until a small group lobbied for its restoration. The condition of the tram was such that the new car will be a replica rather than a restoration. Alan Keef built a new frame for the chassis, though there is still much work to do before the tram can run on the island's railway.

CLOGHER VALLEY RAILWAY 1932 – 1941

The Clogher Valley Tramway was opened in 1887. It ran from Tynan to Maguiresbridge (both Great Northern stations on different lines of that Northern Ireland railway system). However before long the Directors realised that the name tramway restricted their actions, for example as a tramway they could not organise through bookings on other railways for passengers. In 1894 the shareholders adopted the name 'The Clogher Valley Railway Company Limited'. It originally ran with steam locomotives, however, following years of trading losses, the Company sought to

The railcar of the Clogher Valley Railway runs down Fivemiletown main street.

reduce costs in 1932 by purchasing two diesel chassis from Walker Bros. in Wigan. One was used to power a 28 seat coach, turning it into a railcar; the other was used on a two axle open back lorry. The wheels of the lorry were fitted with coupling rods. A small four-wheel van was frequently hauled by the railcar to carry luggage and goods. The two diesel units continued to give service until the system closed in 1941. The railcar was sold to the County Donegal Railway where it ran as number 10 to the closing of the system. It can now be seen as an exhibit at the Ulster Folk and Transport Museum.

The second diesel powered unit on the Clogher Valley Railway was this open back lorry. Note the coupling rods linking the wheels.

QUEEN'S PIER TRAMWAY, RAMSEY 1937 - 1991

The pier in Ramsey was opened to the public on 22nd July 1886. It was constructed with an integral 3ft. gauge tramway track with eight four-wheel luggage trucks. These were propelled by porters taking passengers' luggage to the end of the 2,160ft. long pier, to be loaded onto ferries to the mainland. In 1899 a passenger carriage was added, but everything was still hand propelled. In 1906 the Isle of Man Harbour Board, owners of the pier, seriously considered purchasing a small electric tramcar for passenger use and, possibly, to extend the line to reach the Manx Electric Railway station, however, nothing came of it. Hand propulsion continued until 1937 when a small petrol powered locomotive was purchased from F. C. Hibbard and Company. It was a 'Planet' class 0-4-0 with an 8 hp engine. A ten seat bogie passenger trailer was purchased at the same time. These provided the passenger service until 1950, when a ten seat Wickham petrol tramcar was purchased, powered by a Ford petrol engine. During busy periods both powered vehicles were used, the service being facilitated by a passing loop halfway along the pier. In the 1970s the locomotive was given a face lift to make it appear more like a steam locomotive (though not enough to fool anyone). The Wickham railcar was moved to the Isle of Man Railway in 1975 where it was used to assist lifting track on the disused Peel and Ramsey lines. The work finished in 1978 after which the railcar was scrapped. The locomotive continued to run until 9th September 1981 when the tramway was closed due to the wooden bearers being considered unsafe to take the weight of the locomotive and carriage. They were moved to the Ramsey MER tram shed. In 1989 buildings at the pier head were destroyed in a fire (believed to be caused by vandals) and the pier was closed to the public. Money was invested by the Department of Highways, Ports and Properties (DHPP) into repairing the damage. However, the DHPP stated that they would close the pier if vandalisation continued. Within months there was damage and the pier was closed in June 1991. Despite many attempts to raise money to repair the pier it remains closed. The Planet locomotive and the passenger coach were moved to Jurby when the transport museum opened in 2010 and where they are now on public display.

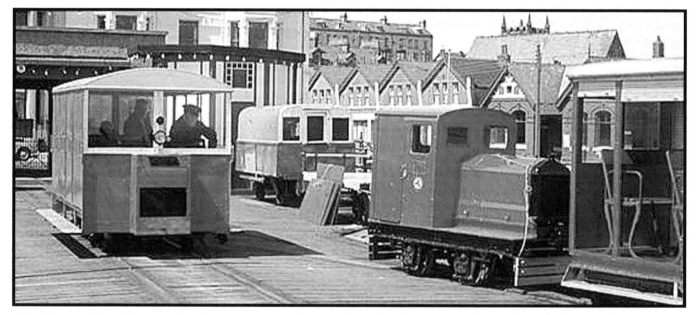

On Queens Pier, Ramsey the two passenger transport units are seen together. The Wickham railcar is ready to leave for the pier end while the locomotive 'Planet' waits in the siding with its passenger trailer.

WALTON-ON-THE-NAZE PIER 1948 - 1978

In 1898 a new pier was opened in Walton-on-the-Naze which replaced a previous structure opened in 1830. The new pier had a 3ft. 6in. electric tramway that ran until 1935 when it was replaced by a rubber tyred battery operated guided coach that ran in a wooden trough. This ran until 30th May 1942 when the pier and the guided coach were destroyed by fire. A new ½ mile pier was built after the war by the local Council that had a contractor's 2ft. gauge light railway. The railway was converted to passenger operation using a locomotive with a petrol engine. Originally built by E. E. Baguley Limited, Burton on Trent in 1939 for R. J. Lakin it had a Ford 24 hp petrol engine and a two speed gearbox. It ran on Wilson's Pleasure Railway at Allhallows-on-Sea, Kent with the as 'No 1 Dreadnought'. The body was made to resemble a steam locomotive.

Petrol power rather than steam, the Walton-on–the-Naze pier locomotive had been given a face, presumably to emulate 'Thomas' from the Rev Awdry's books.

The Walton Pier owners purchased three open, toastrack type, carriages for the railway. The locomotive would pull the coaches to the ends where there were passing loops allowing the locomotive to run around the carriages to pull the carriages for the return journey. It appears to have been well used as in 1952 the Ford engine was replaced with a 24 hp Lister diesel engine and this was replaced in 1972 by an 18 hp Lister diesel. During the latter refurbishment the locomotive was repainted red and black with a 'Thomas the Tank Engine' style face on the 'firebox' door.

The pier was hit by severe storms in January 1978 that damaged the railway. Further storms in the December made it uneconomical to repair the line, so the railway was closed. The locomotive (now called The Lady Guinevere) was sent to Steamtown where it was given a complete overhaul. In 1983 the locomotive and carriages saw further use at Camelot Theme Park, Charnock Richard; then in 1987 it moved to Hewitts Farm, Orpington; and finally to Amerton Railway, Stafford in 1991.

SOUTHPORT PIER 1950 - 1998

The pier at Southport was built in 1860 and was 1,465 yards long, at the time the longest iron pier in the world. It is unusual as for around half of its length it passes over land before it reaches the sea. It was soon realised that some form of transport was needed to carry the public to the head of the pier. A single 3ft. 6in. gauge track was laid along the centre of the decking and the line opened in 1863 with a hand propelled luggage/passenger carriage. This proved such an attraction that the pier owners decided to widen the pier and move the track to one side. This would also enable them to install cable power. The cable operation started in 1865 and is believed to have been the first cable hauled passenger railway in the world. In 1905 the line was converted to electric operation (using DC power from the local town supply) with three 60 seat cars forming a train. By 1936 the pier was in need of renovation and repairs. The Southport Corporation decided to purchase it and new electric carriages were ordered from a local Company. In 1939 the electrical equipment of the cars was replaced, however, in 1950 the electrical supply in the town was changed to AC.

The electric stock was replaced with a 1ft. 11½in. gauge miniature railway. The miniature railway opened on 27th May 1950 with a Hudson-Hunslet 20 hp diesel locomotive that was designed to look like a 4-4-0 steam locomotive. There were five enclosed and ten open carriages made by Kent and Sussex Woodcraft Limited. It seems that the stock was not able to meet its demands as in 1953 it was replaced by two diesel powered units, four open carriages and one enclosed, all the vehicles having bogies and run as a single train. The blue and silver train was named 'Silver

Belle' with raised letters at each end. There was a serious derailment in 1970 that damaged the train and track, forcing the line to close for the remainder of the season. The Council decided that the 'Silver Belle' was too old to repair. After consideration it was decided to repair the track and, as the power units were reassessed two of the more damaged open carriages and the enclosed carriage were scrapped and a short train of the remaining stock was used when the line reopened on 18th March 1971. Soon it was decided to replace the rolling stock and a new locomotive and four bogie carriages (one enclosed and three open) were purchased from Severn Lamb in 1973. The locomotive was a bogie diesel-electric and named 'English Rose'. Apart from a brief interruption in the mid-1990s, the train ran until 1998 when the pier was declared in need of urgent repairs. The railway rolling stock was sold, one locomotive and two enclosed carriages went to the West Lancashire Railway, the other locomotive and five carriages were sold to the Moseley Railway Trust. The pier lay closed for four years, reopening in 2002, but without a tramway. A new tramway was installed, with a battery operated, articulated tram, in 2005. The battery operated service continued to run, even though the tramcar had to be left in the open during the nights, as there was no shelter for it. The new service seemed over the top. The articulated three bogie tramcar was far too large for the job it was asked to do. Manufactured by UK Loco Limited the car seated 74 with a body length of 22m. (70ft.) and a width of 2.4m. (8ft.). The pier was reasonably short at ¾ mile long, easily walked in ten minutes, possibly much less as there is also access from the car park half way along the pier. As a result, the service was very lightly trafficked. Rising maintenance costs meant it ran at a loss and so the Council decided to cease the service in June 2015 in order to save money. The tram was sent for scrap and an existing rubber tyred land train now provides the passenger service, as its route includes calling at places outside the pier.

The 'Silver Belle' running on Southport Pier before its derailment led to it being withdrawn.

SNAEFELL MOUNTAIN RAILWAY 1951 - DATE

The summit of Snaefell houses not only the terminus of the Snaefell Mountain Railway and the summit café, it also houses a building belonging to the Civil Aviation Authority containing transmitter masts for aircraft and island communication. CAA staff need to access the equipment for maintenance and repairs. When the railway is running it is used to take staff to the summit. However, the railway service ceases out of season and the overhead wire above the bungalow is removed for the winter. In order to continue access the CAA have maintained a number of small railcars. The accommodation for the railcars is located by the railway shed at Laxey.

The first CAA railcar was purchased by the Manx Electric Railway for use on the Snaefell line. After serving 12 years as the line's ancillary vehicle it was retired and left next to the depot, where it deteriorated until being privately purchased and shipped to England.

The first was purchased by the Air Ministry (predecessor of the CAA) in 1951 from Wickham of Ware (works number 5864). Logically it was given the number 1, though this was not displayed on the car. It had a Ford V8 petrol engine driving a four-wheel chassis that was fitted with a central Fell brake. Shelter was provided in the form of a small depot close to the SMR shed. In 1965 the petrol engine was removed and a diesel engine put in its place. It continued in service until 1977 when it was decided to retire it. Now surplus to requirements, number 1 was sold to the Manx Electric Railway (owners of the Snaefell Mountain Railway). It became a works vehicle for the SMR, a role it carried out until the 1980s when it was retired to rest outside the SMR shed. The elements were not kind to it and it rusted badly and deteriorated with parts being removed. The derelict body was sold to a private individual in June 2007 and it was moved back to England. It is now at the Statfold Barn Railway, Staffordshire, where it is waiting for future restoration.

The newest CAA railcar is number 4, purchased in 1991. Photograph Gordon Astill.

Number 2 (works number 7642) was built in 1957 by Wickham of Ware with a diesel engine to join number 1 to give a choice of two cars, one being active the other as reserve (roles they swapped regularly). This continued until number 1 was sold to the SMR in 1977, when number 2 was joined by number 3. The pair continued to share the duties until 1991 when number 2 went back to Wickham of Ware. Back at its manufacturer number 2 was given a complete overhaul and is believed to have been sold to South Africa.

Number 3 (works number 10956, another diesel) arrived from Wickham of Ware in 1977 having been purchased by the National Air Traffic Services (predecessor to the CAA). With number 2 it shared the duties until 1991 when number 4 replaced number 2. Number 3 continues to give service. In 1991 number 4 (works number 11730) was purchased, again from Wickham of Ware. It also has a diesel engine and is longer than the previous cars as it has an open loading area at one end. With number 3 it is still in service.

WISBECH AND UPWELL TRAMWAY 1952 - 1966

The Wisbech and Upwell Tramway initially opened between Wisbech and Outwell in 1883 with distinctive steam locomotives (immortalised by Toby the Tram Engine in the books by Rev. W. Awdry). The extension to Upwell was opened in the following year. The line was authorised as a tramway, using the provisions of the 1870 Tramways Act. and the track was laid alongside the roadway, without any fencing. The principal use of the line was to move fruit and vegetables quickly from the farms to the markets in London. In addition to this seasonal work the line also provided a passenger service until the end of 1927.

Drewry diesel locomotive number 11102, one of two allocated to the Wisbech and Upwell Tramway.

After the Second World War railways were exploring the use of diesel locomotives for shunting and branch line duties. The Drewry Car Company were commissioned to build thirteen diesel-mechanical 0-6-0 locomotives for use on dock lines and the Wisbech branch. The East Anglian lines were to have four locomotives (actually built by the Vulcan Foundry) that were equipped with side valances, hiding the wheels. Two of them, numbered 11102 and 11103, were allocated to the Wisbech branch. They started in service in August 1952, though teething problems meant that one of the steam locomotives was kept in reserve for nine months. Later 11103 was transferred to docks duties and was replaced by 11101. In the late 1950s they were renumbered 11101 to D2201 and 11102 to D2202 and given the class '04'. The goods service continued until the line closed on 23rd May 1966. The two locomotives went to shunting duties at Crewe works, being scrapped and broken up in 1968.

BLACKPOOL TRAMWAYS 1958 - Date

The Blackpool tramway is the only tramway in the British Isles that has developed from a traditional tramway to a modern system. In essence it provides a link between the historical and the new and the tramway recognises this by running a heritage service in the holiday season, mixing preserved tramcars with the modern fleet. One of the developments that the tramway has seen is the use of road-rail vehicles for maintenance and repairs of its infrastructure. In addition to dedicated works tramcars (including converted cars that reached the end of their passenger life) since 1982 there have been a number of road-rail works vehicles. Essentially road lorries, they have been fitted with small metal guide wheels that run along the rails ensuring that the rubber tyred wheels keep to the top of the rails. All the other mechanical elements of the vehicles remain in situ. This has allowed tramways to move works equipment quickly by road and then, if necessary, onto reserved track. In Blackpool much of the track is open sleepered on its own right of way. If a tram becomes disabled the road-rail vehicles can drive on the road, passing tramcars unable to proceed because of the obstruction, then put itself on the track to reach the stricken tram. In addition the tramway has had dedicated works trams and trailers, most of which are outside the scope of this book. However, two of them were equipped with diesel engines to enable them to be driven when the overhead power is switched off. These are the first cars to be described.

In 1958 the standard type tramcars were reaching the ends of their lives and many were headed for the scrap heap. One car, number 143, was selected for further duties as a works car. The car was converted to an open top condition so that a tower could be erected on the upper deck to allow engineers access to the overhead. A PD2 diesel engine was mounted in the lower saloon driving a generator that produced enough electricity to either drive the car or, when linked to

Engineering car number 753 was often parked at Little Bispham turning circle, ready to attend any incident that may occur on the line.

the overhead wire, to provide power to dead sections to allow other tramcars to be driven. When it entered service as an engineering car it was renumbered 3, later to become 753. In addition to scheduled maintenance the car was used in emergencies and to facilitate this aspect of its role it was kept at the front of the depot. Over the years its appearance gradually deteriorated. Early in the morning of 30th June 1990 the tram was on its way to undertake emergency overhead repairs at Broadwater when a fire broke out inside the saloon. It was fierce enough to require

The current engineering car is number 754 that was purpose built in 1992.

attendance of the fire brigade. The car was badly damaged and the car was towed back to the depot. It was decided that the car was too damaged to economically repair it and a new overhead line car was ordered. No 753 was removed and is being restored back to its original passenger condition by the Lancastrian Transport Trust and Blackpool Transport.

The car that replaced 753 was the first purpose built overhead line car that the Blackpool Tramway has had. Entering service in 1992 with the number 754, the tramcar was built by East Lancashire Coachbuilders, Blackburn. Like 753, 754 was fitted with a Leyland 0.600 diesel engine driving a generator, so it was able to drive on the tramway when the overhead power was switched off. The new car brought a modern body design with similarities to 761 and 762. It has had an uneventful service and continues as a vital member of the maintenance fleet.

In 1982 the tramway purchased a versatile overhead repair vehicle, a Mercedes Benz Unimog. Numbered 440 (registration number YFV 557Y) for the fleet, this diesel powered lorry could operate as a normal rubber tyred vehicle on the road and the paved section of the tramway. The Unimog was fitted with small steel wheels that enabled the lorry to run along the rails. It could fulfil a number of functions, taking engineers to disabled tramcars and broken overhead. If tramcars could not be repaired, the Unimog was able to tow the tramcar back to the depot for more extensive repairs. It was renumbered to 940 in 1996 and continued to give service until around 2005.

Another road/rail overhead repair lorry was acquired from Bedford/Bruff in 1987. It carried number 441 (registration number D801 CTP)

There are other members of the works fleet that have diesel engines. One is the Mercedes Benz Unimog, number 939 (J271 TEC) acquired second hand in 2003, and going into service the following year, this lorry, like 940, has steel railway guide wheels that can be lowered onto the rails to guide the vehicle while the rubber wheels give the power. In the usual Unimog style the drive, whether on the road or on rails is a diesel engine. It has a platform on the end of a raising arm that can lift engineers to work on the overhead. The vehicle continues giving service reaching repairs on the reserved section of the line and rescuing disabled tramcars.

The Mercedes Benz Unimog, number 440 (YFV 557Y) rescues a derailed Brush railcoach. Sand had been blown from the beach onto the track causing the tramcar to leave the rails. The tramcar was carefully towed back onto the rails and it made its own way back to the depot.

Using its rail guidance wheels, engineering car number 938 (Q204 HFR) undertakes overhead maintenance work near the North Pier.

Finally there is another specialist works lorry with a tower platform. It was purchased from Midland Metro in 2005 and given the number 938 with the unusual registration number of Q204 HFR. It has a left hand drive (there is a warning notice on the back of the vehicle warning other road users of this). It has a box shaped body giving a shelter to the engineers in inclement weather and protects their tools and equipment. It is still in service. In addition to the above, a further diesel engine rail vehicle appeared at Blackpool. This was a Speno Railgrinder HRR 12-M1 that had been hired in the 1990s by Blackpool Tramways to remove rail corrugations. When special work has been contracted out it is common for the contractors to use their own vehicles, some of which are similar road-rail lorries to those already described. However, these are all transitory and are not within the scope of this volume.

Looking very ungainly Unimog 939 enters the private right of way south of Lord Street, Fleetwood

SHEFFIELD CORPORATION TRAMWAYS 1960

The Sheffield Tramways ceased running in 1960 and the majority of the tramcars were sold for scrap. One of Thomas William Ward's scrapyards (Ward was a major ship breaker and scrap merchant) was close to Tynsley depot. A temporary track was laid to enable the redundant tramcars to be pushed to the yard to be broken up. A diesel lorry was used to move the cars, however, it is not known if this vehicle was part of the tram fleet or if it was owned by the breaker.

NATIONAL TRAMWAY MUSEUM, CRICH 1963 - DATE

Early in the development of the Tramway Museum Society site at Crich tram track was laid, however, there was no overhead or electricity generating plant. To enable volunteers to have tramway rides the museum used a local horse to haul a horse tram for special occasions. The only other form of railed power was 'John Bull' the steam tram locomotive. The fledgling tramway collection occasionally required to be moved around and this was achieved by brute force and crowbars. The answer came in the form of a 60cm narrow gauge diesel built by Ruston Hornsby in 1944. Its initial history is not known, but by 1963 it was owned by George Cohen Limited of Leeds. David Renard, the son of the Works Manager, had an interest in the Tramway Museum and informed his father that the museum needed motive power and they set about re-gauging the little locomotive to 4ft. 8½in. It was delivered to the museum in the Summer of 1963. Clearly not everyone was enamoured by the diesel as it was disparagingly called 'phut-phut' in 'The Journal'. Running boards were fitted over the wheels for safety. Initially it carried the identification 'TMS' painted on the sides. At a much later date it was given the name 'Rupert' (the nickname of David

Renard). The locomotive continues to be part of the museum fleet, but these days more as an exhibit than a working vehicle.

In 1969 the museum purchased a second diesel-mechanical shunter. This was a Ruston Hornsby 0-4-0 diesel that was re-gauged from metre gauge to 4ft. 8½in. in order to run on the museum tramway. The history of this locomotive is fascinating. Built in 1952 by Ruston Hornsby the locomotive was destined for the metre gauge Clay Cross Company industrial railway at Crich. It joined a similar locomotive purchased the previous year. The first locomotive was named 'Ted' after the quarry manager, the second locomotive was given the name 'G.M.J.' after the husband of Dowie (the nickname given to the Company chairman's daughter-in-law). The quarry was closed in 1957 and the railway stock was taken to the Company's lime works in Ambergate. The locomotive was involved in a fire in 1963 and was declared derelict and was relegated to a siding. When the tramway museum required another locomotive to support 'Rupert' the management team approached the Company. A working locomotive was beyond the limited resources of the museum, but the derelict 'G.M.J.' was affordable. An inspection revealed that the damage caused by the fire and exposure to the elements was all repairable. It was transferred to the museum site and restored to working condition by volunteers, retaining its name. It continued in service with a special event in 1999. This was the fortieth anniversary of the start of the Crich tramway, when a group from the Tramway Museum Society visited the Crich quarry and decided to purchase the land as the site for the museum. It was felt that the occasion should be celebrated with a trip on horse car 15 hauled by the works diesel 'G.M.J.' (that did work in the quarry). However, when the inspection took place the locomotive used was 'Ted' (similar to G.M.J.) so for the anniversary the locomotive was given a temporary nameplate of 'Ted' (see below). At the end of the event 'G.M.J.' was given back its proper nameplate.

Two of the diesel shunters at Crich. The first to arrive at Crich is on the left, 'Rupert', while on the right is 'GMC'. Both clearly show their conversion from narrow gauge to standard gauge.

At the time of purchasing 'G.M.J.', 'Ted' was also for sale, however, as a running locomotive it was too expensive for the museum. The Clay Cross Company failed to sell 'Ted' and it was left unused in the works yard. Later the museum was able to purchase the now derelict 'Ted' as a source of spare parts for 'G.M.J.' It was transferred to Clay Cross store where parts were removed as and when needed to keep 'G.M.J.' going. 'Ted' was moved to the museum site in February 2004 for dismantling, with useful parts being kept in store and the remainder scrapped.

Sheffield number 349 gained publicity as an illuminated car on the last tram procession in 1960 seeing the end of that city's trams (until the opening of the new generation of tramways in 1994). Number 349 was not scrapped, but went to the National Tramway Museum, Crich. In the early days of the museum there was no generating station and in 1964 349 was fitted with a petrol engine driving a generator allowing it to be driven along the track before the overhead was erected. It was also given a new number, 01; once the museum gained its overhead 349 became a

No photograph has been found of Blackpool railgrinder number 2 at Crich. Here is a photograph of it before leaving Blackpool.

generator car, supplying power to enable other tramcars to run on the museum site. In 1967 it suffered a 'flash-over' damaging the electrical equipment. The museum considered that the body of the car was beyond economic repair and so it was withdrawn and the petrol-generator was removed for servicing and installation in the ex-Blackpool rail grinder, number 2. The body of number 01 was scrapped while the truck was used under Blackpool number 2.

To replace the generator car Blackpool number 2, a railgrinder, was selected. This works car had been acquired in the early 1960s when Blackpool tramway had declared it redundant. The initial purpose was to reclaim electrical equipment to restore Manchester 765. Following the damage to 01 (described above), after refurbishment the generator equipment was installed in number 2 (renumbered 02) and it became the museum reserve source of electrical power as well as being able to move when the main current was switched off. Eventually the public electrical supply was guaranteed and lack of space on the museum site led to it being taken to Clay Cross for storage.

Ex-Tramlink works car number 058 parked in the depot yard at Crich.

When works car rail crane 058 and truck 061 became surplus to Croydon Tramlink's requirements in 2010 they were sold to the National Tramway Museum. They arrived at the museum on 19th January 2010 and joined the works fleet, as well as being exhibits themselves. In 2016 number 058 has been named by the museum, 'John Gardner' after a member of the society who worked hard during the early years of the museum to help create the popular attraction it now is.

EAST ANGLIA TRANSPORT MUSEUM 1966 – DATE

The site of the East Anglia Transport Museum was first developed in 1965. It now has an extensive collection of trolleybuses and six tramcars, with a length of track to enable them to be run and give visitors the opportunity to have a ride. Of interest to this book is a preserved London Transport ancillary vehicle in the permanent collection. This is a Fordson petrol tractor that was used to move trams, trolleybuses and buses around depots and repair workshops. It has the fleet number 626X but was not registered for use on the public highway. If it did need to venture out it would be fitted with trade plates. It entered service in 1942 and was withdrawn in 1966, when it was purchased by the Uxbridge and District Vintage Vehicle Society for preservation. They presented it to the East Anglia Transport Museum in 1967. It has been extensively restored and is on display at the museum. On special event days it may be joined by a similar tractor, number 351X (registration number CUC 192) that is in private ownership.

The Fordson petrol tractor, number 626X restored and preserved at the East Anglia Transport Museum. Note the solid rubber tyres and the large padded buffers to minimise any damage to the vehicles being pushed by the tractor.

SEATON AND DISTRICT ELECTRIC TRAMWAY 1973 – DATE

When Modern Electric Tramways moved from Eastbourne to Seaton, the new line ran from the depot to Bobsworth Bridge. The line was extended to Colyton in 1971. Then the opportunity rose to link the tramway with the car park near Seaton town centre when the local farmer agreed to sell a strip of land to the tramway. In order to prepare the track bed a thousand tons of brick rubble was bought from a local brickworks to create a slope from the depot to the track bed at the side of the field. To assist moving the rubble into place in 1973 a Ruston and Hornsby diesel shunter (number 435398) was purchased second-hand from the North Devon Clay Company. Regauged by the tramway from 3ft. to 2ft. 9in. the locomotive was used for all kinds of engineering duties. Demand for its services gradually diminished and it spent much of its latter years parked on the siding at Colyton. Then a Kubota tractor was purchased and 435398 was sold to the Devon Railway Centre, Bickleigh.

Left: Allan and Sue Gardner on the Ruston Hornsby diesel number 435398.

The Kubota tractor in the Seaton depot with works trailers front and back.

The Kubota tractor arrived in 2002 and was equipped for road/rail operation. It has a shovel bucket at the front and a narrow bucket at the back. The vehicle is fitted with small steel wheels that can be lowered to run on the tramway rails, the rubber wheels being suitable for the 2ft. 9in. gauge. The ability to run on either road or rail track makes it far more versatile than 435398 it replaced.

COTSWOLD MARINA TRAMWAY, SOUTH CERNEY 1973 – c1980

A boating and leisure complex opened in the Cotswolds, near South Cerney. To serve the centre a metre gauge, one-mile-long tramway was built between the car park and the main facilities. To provide transport for the public three tram trailers were purchased second hand from the Charleroi Tramway, Belgium. Retaining their Charleroi livery, the tram trailers were hauled by a small petrol locomotive that had been purchased second hand from the docks at Gibraltar. The centre was somewhat remote and the tramway was not heavily used. Sometime around 1980 it was closed and the tram trailers were sold to Shane's Railway, Northern Ireland.

The three ex Charleroi trailers working on the Cotswold Marina Tramway in 1972.

FURTHER READING

MCEWAN PRATT AND COMPANY

The Engineer: 19th November 1920 page 513

KENT AND EAST SUSSEX

Commercial Motor: 22nd December 1922

THE SHROPSHIRE AND MONTGOMERSHIRE RAILWAY

The Shropshire & Montgomeryshire Light Railway by Peter Johnson , published by Oxford Publishing Co., 2008

THE SELSEY TRAMWAY

The Selsey Tram: by David Bathurst, published by Phillimore & Co., 1992
The Selsey Tramway Vols 1 & 2: by Laurie A. Cooksey, published by Wild Swan Publications, 2006

CASTLEBERG AND VICTORIA BRIDGE TRAMWAY

The Castleberg and Victoria Bridge Tramway: by Dr E. M. Patterson, published by Colourpoint Books

HERNE BAY PIER

Pier Railways and Tramways of the British Isles: by Keith Turner, published by Oakwood press, second edition 1999.

.RYDE PIER TRAMWAY

Pier Railways and Tramways of the British Isles: by Keith Turner, published by The Oakwood Press, second edition 1999.
The Piers, Tramways and Railways at Ryde: by R. J. Maycock and R. Silsbury, published by The Oakwood Press, 2005.

CLOGHER VALLEY RAILWAY

The Clogher Valley Railway: by Edward M. Patterson, published by David & Charles, 1972.

QUEEN'S PIER TRAMWAY, RAMSEY

Isle of Man Tramways: by F. K. Pearson, published by David and Charles, 1970.
Pier Railways and Tramways of the British Isles: by Keith Turner, published by The Oakwood Press, second edition 1999.
Rails in the Isle of Man, A Colour Celebration: by Robert Hendry, published by Midland Publishing Limited, 1993
Isle of Man Tramways: by Norman Jones, published by Foxline Publishing, 1994

CHAPTER 5

MODERN TIMES

MANX ELECTRIC RAILWAY 1978 – DATE

The history of the use of petrol and diesel power on the Manx Electric Railway (MER) is not entirely straightforward. The vehicles using internal combustion power fall into two camps. There are diesel works railcars that are owned by the Isle of Man Railway (IMR) that are shared between them and the MER. This is possible because the two railways have a common gauge of 3ft. (unlike the Sneafell Mountain Railway that has a 3ft. 6in. gauge). The other works railmotors are a series of visitors, owned by private contractors (mostly by RMS Locotec that has been contracted to carry out much maintenance and reconstruction work on both railways).

The four diesel powered units that are shared are two Wickham and two Simplex railmotors . The Wickham units were purchased in 1978 and were ex-Lochaber Railway, a 3ft. gauge industrial railway in Scotland that closed in 1973. The railmotors had been stored at Possil Park, Glasgow until sold to IMR. They have both been given unofficial numbers, 22 and 23. Number 22 (Wickham works number 7442) was built in 1956. In addition to its use as an engineer's inspection and repair trolley it has appeared on special occasions such as the MER 'Centenary of Electric Traction' in 1979 and is currently based at Derby Castle Depot. The other Wickham is number 23 (Wickham works number 8849) built in 1961. Like number 22 it has made a number of appearances at MER events, though it is normally shedded at Douglas Station. In 1966 the Motor Rail Company (Simplex) built a diesel mechanical 0-4-0 locomotive with the works number 40S280 for the National Coal Board pit at Kilnhurst, Yorkshire. It was purchased by the MER in October 1996. In 2009 it was repainted yellow (gaining the nickname 'Yellow Peril') with the letters 'MER' on each side. It has been used on the MER and the IMR for engineering duties and it has appeared at a variety of events on the MER. It is currently at Douglas in the steam railway sheds. Another Motor Rail Simplex locomotive is on the island. Built in 1959 with the works number 22021 it was destined for B&S Massey's forge in Cheshire. It was purchased second hand in 1983 by the IMR and moved to the island where it was stored for many years in Douglas engine shed. After a complete overhaul it was used on the MER on event days. In 2009 it went back to the MER to assist in the relocation of cars from Homefield Bus Garage where they had been in temporary storage. Currently it is back on the IMR as the Port Erin carriage shed shunter.

The 1988 ex-Lochaber Railway Wickham railcars, number 7442 (left, seen on the MER and parked at the Douglas terminus) and number 8849 (right, in the Isle of Man Railways sheds). Photographs; left Phil Parker, 1959 and right TLRS collection.

Simplex locomotive 22021 that was purchased second hand and arrived on the Isle of Man in 1983.

The following locomotives and railmotors have worked or are still working on the MER at various times, some having journeyed to and from the island on several occasions. The precise history of each vehicle's visits is not clear, however, each had spent some time on the island.

The first of the visiting locomotives was 'Bertie', a Ruston and Hornsby diesel mechanical locomotive (works number 281290). It was built in 1949 and sold to the Associated Portland Cement Manufacturers, Warwickshire, for work at the Ufton Lime pits in Warwickshire. After a spell at Kilvington Gypsum in Nottinghamshire it was donated to Northamptonshire Locomotive Group in December 1984, going to the Irchester Narrow Gauge Museum. It was loaned to RMS Locotec who shipped it to the island in 2006 for use as part of their permanent way fleet with the number HO48. It has carried out passenger duties hauling tram trailer 62 for events in 2008. No longer required it was taken off the island in 2010 and returned to the Weardale Railway.

The well travelled Ruston and Hornsby locomotive 'Bertie' that visited the island in 2006 and stayed for a few years.

A diesel mechanical 0-4-0 locomotive, built by the Motor Rail Company in 1980, was purchased from the Bord na Mona by RMS Locotec in 2008. It has a Lister HR4 air cooled diesel engine and the unattractive name 'Pig'. It has made a number of visits to the Island starting in 2008, with the final being in 2015 and it remains in service on the MER. Like the other two locomotives it has participated in many of the special events run by the MER.

A Dundalk Engineering diesel locomotive (works number LM363) was supplied to the Bord na Mona in 1984 and subsequently purchased by RMS Locotec in February 2009. It was sent for use on the island soon after purchase and stayed for a little over a year, leaving in November 2010 and is currently stored at the Weardale Railway.

SHANE'S CASTLE RAILWAY, NORTHERN IRELAND c1980 – 1995

In 1971 Lord O'Neill opened a 3ft. gauge railway to take visitors from the estate entrance to the ruins of Shane's Castle (burnt down in 1816). Around 1980 three ex-Charleroi tram trailers were purchased from the Cotswolds Marina, that no longer required them. The railway had a mixture of steam and diesel locomotives so the trailers would have been pulled by the most convenient (available) locomotive. The railway closed in 1995 and the tram trailers put up for sale. They were purchased by the Fintown Railway in County Donegal.

TYNE AND WEAR METRO 1980 – 2005

The building of the Tyne and Wear Metro started in 1974 and the first line opened in August 1980. In 1976, prior to the opening of the line, five 0-6-0 diesel-electric shunters were purchased from Brush Electric Machines Limited (works numbers 801 – 805) to assist in the construction (though it is thought that they were not delivered until 1979). On the Metro they were given the numbers WL1 to WL5. They had Rolls Royce DV8N 427 bhp engines driving through Brush electrical gear and were capable of reaching 31 mph. Construction of the system continued for many more years and the diesel locomotives continued to assist. They were also used as shunters to move stock around the depots, moving works trailers and recovering disabled trains in emergencies. In November 1991 they were declared surplus to requirements and all were sold to the Channel Tunnel construction contract and renumbered 60 to 64 (but not in works number order). It had been decided to replace the works locomotives with three new Hunslet battery-electric shunters (capable of operating either from the overhead or using their own battery power and numbered BL1, BL2 and BL3).

Just two of the Tyne and Wear Metro diesel locomotives have survived, numbers WL3 and WL4. The latter is currently part of the collection of the Great Eastern Traction, Norfolk. Photograph Roger Monk.

When their work on the tunnel ended, they were sold to Insulated Structures to work at the Round Oak Steelworks, Dudley. However, they were asked to do duties beyond their capacity and after being overloaded they were withdrawn from service for scrapping. Locomotive WL3 suffered a fire in 2005 and was subsequently sold as scrap to Andrew Briddon, who rather than cut it up added it as a static member of his collection of locomotives and is held at Peak Rail. WL4 was acquired by Great Eastern Traction and is now in storage. The other three locomotives have been scrapped.

SOUTHEND PIER 1986 – DATE

The iron Southend pier was opened in 1889 replacing the original wooden structure. A 3ft. 6in. electric tramway was opened in 1890. The new pier was extended in 1898 when a new pier head was added to overcome silting up of the channel. Other extensions were added in 1927 and 1929. It is now 1½ miles long and is well known as the longest pier of the British Isles. The forty-year-old crossbench rolling stock was replaced with modern electric cars in 1949. In 1975 work began on extensive renewal and renovations. As part of the rebuilding a special Atlas/PAPE 500SP self-propelled, hydraulic crane was purchased from Papes Advanced Project Engineers Limited. The crane worked along the rails and when it was required to lift heavy items the wheel would retract and the bottom of the vehicle rested along the rails, evenly distributing the weight. Another vehicle arrived on the pier in February 1976, a petrol driven Wickham 4-wheel personnel carrier. In the same year there was a major fire at the pier head which caused extensive damage. During the renovation work it was discovered that the tramway track and signalling were unsafe and first the east track was closed to passenger use then at the beginning of October 1978 the whole line was closed. The carriages were scheduled for scrapping, but a few were saved and are now static exhibits in the Pier Museum and a local shop.

The land end station on the Southend Pier Railway with both trains. The train in service is towing a flat wagon, used for taking goods to the facilities at the end of the pier.

It was not until 1985 that construction of the new railway was started. Contractors May Gurney (Colchester) Limited started laying a 3ft. gauge single track line with a passing loop at the half-way point and double tracks at the stations. To help in the construction the contractors brought their own four-wheel diesel works car. It was used to move construction material up the line. It is unsure how long the unit was kept on the pier. The new pier tramway opened on 2nd May 1986 with two seven bogie car units built by Severn Lamb Engineering Company of Stratford-upon-Avon. The power unit in each train is a 55 hp Deutz diesel engine with a hydraulic drive to the axles. The units are named 'Sir John Betjeman' and 'Sir William Heygate' and each has a capacity of 175 persons. There was an embarrassing episode when an official party, including the Mayor of Southend, was travelling to officially open the rebuilt pier head station on 17th September 2009. The leading unit derailed near the halfway loop. Since then the line has operated well.

In 1996 a smaller, three axle railcar, made by Castleline of Nottingham, was purchased that could carry 26 passengers and was battery operated (hence not of direct interest to this book). The idea was to use it on quieter winter days. It was given the number 1835, the year the first wooden pier opened. In fact it has not been used for public transport with its main use being to move staff and goods up and down the line.

DOCKLANDS LIGHT RAILWAY 1987 - DATE

The first diesel to be used on the Docklands Light Railway was a Wickham crane trolley type CT30 (DLR number 992). This was used to assist in the track construction leading up to the opening of the railway in 1987. It was a four wheel vehicle with an open platform that had a crane. The trolley was given the name 'Sooty'. There are two possible reasons, the first is a corruption of the 'CT' of its type classification, the other referred to the smoke and fumes emitted when it started from cold. The name was so popular that it was given an official name plate. There is no record of when it was withdrawn, though it is likely that once all the initial lines had been opened, by 1994, it would no longer have had a use and would have been sold. A Ruston and Hornsby diesel locomotive was purchased second hand that was able to rescue broken down trains. This was an 0-4-0 shunter built in 1962 by Ruston and Hornsby of Lincoln and it joined the Docklands Light Railway just before the railway opened in 1987. Originally numbered by the DLR as 95, (later renumbered 995). Based at the Poplar Depot, it continued giving service until withdrawn in 2009 when it was purchased as a non-working locomotive by the Epping Ongar Railway (EOR). The EOR had another Ruston and Hornsby diesel locomotive of the same design and had purchased the DLR locomotive to salvage it for spares. It was then scrapped.

The GEC second-hand diesel locomotive built in 1979 for Shotton Steelworks, it was acquired by the DLR in 2009 and is based at Poplar depot.

To replace 995 a secondhand GEC Traction 0-4-0 diesel locomotive was purchased in 2009 This locomotive had been one of three built in 1979 for the Shotton Steelworks, near Chester. It is based at the Poplar Depot and has been given the number 994 and the name 'Kevin Keaney' and it continues to work as part of the maintenance fleet. Also in the fleet is a battery operated locomotive, however, that is outside the scope of this book.

The Docklands Light Railway makes extensive use of external contractors for their maintenance and development work. The contractors are expected to provide their own equipment to meet the contractual agreements. As all of the lines are built on their own right of way, much of which is elevated, they require many road-rail vehicles. When work is carried out these vehicles can be seen on or near the line.

A road-rail Contractor BCL Rail Services Limited mechanical shovel parked under the Docklands Light Railway elevated track.

Nearby was a flat bed rail trailer used by the mechanical shovel for moving material.

BLACKPOOL NORTH PIER 1991 - 2004

Blackpool North Pier was completed in 1863 and for most of its life has not had a tramway. It was only when the pier underwent repairs and refurbishment following storm damage in the winter of 1990-1991 that the owners, First Leisure, had the idea of bringing a new image to the pier and they contracted a Company called Beresford Sherman to advise on the reconstruction. One idea that the Company came up with was the installation of a tramway on the pier in particular to take customers to the end of the pier theatre and other attractions, the idea being to provide a sheltered environment (there were passenger shelters at the termini of the tramway) from the often wet days. Chris Renehan, the Australian designer, explained that he went to Tower Models and purchased a plastic model kit of a 'Blackpool Standard tram' of the post 1931 vestibule type (presumably the Hadfields kit). He then built it as a single deck car, mounted it on a model of a section of pier, and it was presented to the board of First Leisure. They approved it and construction went ahead.

On a rather dull day, the location is self evident from the Tower (and the name on the side of the tram). It ran for 13 years before being scrapped.

The three car unit was built by Harry Steer Engineering of Breaston, Derbyshire (a company that specialises in fairground rides). It was 3ft. gauge with each car having bogies with 300mm diameter wheels. The cars were unusual in having a single longitudinal bench seat and doors only on the north side of the cars. The total capacity of the unit was 28 seated and 28 standing. The central car carried the Perkins 2.3 litre diesel engine driving a Linde variable displacement hydraulic pump that powered eight axles (four on the central car and two on each outer car). Each outer car also had disc brakes on all four axles, these were applied by springs that were held off by hydraulic pressure. Driving controls were provided at each end, the one in use automatically deactivated the other. There were also interlocks to prevent any movement if the doors were not closed and the dead man's foot pedal depressed. Public service began on 2nd September 1991. The idea of providing a transport service on the pier may have seemed a good idea to the owners, but the paying public much preferred the (fairly short) walk to spending money. At the end of the 2004 season the tram was removed from the pier. When questioned in 2005 pier staff said it had been removed for repairs and refurbishment. However, it transpired that the unit had gone to be scrapped and the pier tram service permanently ceased.

MANCHESTER METROLINK 1991 - DATE

While the Metrolink was under construction in 1991 a diesel works vehicle was acquired to assist in the building of the line. Since then it has continued to give service on the tramway (the first line opened for public service 6th April 1992). Built by RFS Industries, Kilnhurst, Rotherham it has a Caterpillar diesel-electric unit providing 170 Kw to power its electric motors. It is used on all kinds of works duties throughout the ever expanding system. One important duty has been to carry out gauge tests with new stock and on new routes. With the former it is essential that all the track clearances are checked when a new specification of tramcar is delivered. The diesel vehicle pulls and pushes the tramcar along slowly to ensure that there is sufficient clearance at platforms and that there are no obstructions to strike the tram body. On new routes it is necessary to check each different type of car and here it is useful to have the diesel vehicle as it can carry out testing when the overhead supply is not completed or is switched off. It is fitted with a hydraulic crane enabling it to load and unload heavy material from a works flat truck. Though now over 27 years old it continues to give service. In addition to this lorry there have been a number of other road-rail vehicles used by contractors when extending or maintaining the tramway.

The Manchester Metrolink works car at the Open Day in 1994. It is in its original livery that has since been changed.

A Balfour Beatty contractor's road-rail lorry also at the Metrolink Open Day.

DOUGLAS HORSE TRAMWAY 1993 – DATE

It was a surprise to find that the Douglas Horse Tramway came within the ambit of this book. Later the use of Land Rover vehicles to haul the restored cable car is mentioned, but the first use of petrol power was in three horse trams that were fitted with petrol generators. The reason was not for motive power, all tramcars continued to be hauled by horse, but to provide electricity for illuminations. In 1993 tramcar 43 was illuminated, given a (fake) trolley pole and renumbered to 14 (tramcar 14 is a double deck tramcar currently displayed in the Manx Museum). At the 1993 Douglas Town Carnival the tramcar was dressed to represent what the tram could have looked like had the tramway been converted for electrical operation (as had been suggested at various times in the past). To keep up the appearance it was moved, not by a horse, but by volunteers from the public pushing it along. It was even given a new owner's name 'Manx Electric Railway'.

Above: tramcar number 43, renumbered 14, with its fake trolley pole being pushed by volunteers along the Douglas promenade in 1993.

Left: in 1996 numbers 36 and 43 were illuminated to celebrate the centenary of the Corporation. While 43 reverted to its non illuminated state when the year was over, number 36 continued as an illuminated car into the 2000s.

In 1996 Douglas Corporation celebrated its Centenary and to mark the occasion two horse tramcars, numbers 36 and 43 (this time carrying their own numbers), were illuminated. Like the previous occasion the power for the lights came from a petrol generator fitted below the seats at one end of the car. Light bulbs were attached to the outside of the car, around the windows and had "1896 1996" above the ends and "DOUGLAS 100 YEARS" along the sides of the roof. The cars worked on the promenade service along with other tramcars. To appear at their best they usually worked late afternoon and evenings. Number 43 had its illuminations removed in 1997 while number 36 retained its decorations, though with the reference to the Centenary removed. It was noted to be still illuminated in 2008, though some time after this the decorations were removed. In 2011 tramcar number 1 was selected to be decorated with lights for work on the December Santa Specials running on three days leading up to Christmas. This proved very popular and the event has continued each year since, with number 1 retaining its illuminations throughout the year.

ULSTER FOLK AND TRANSPORT MUSEUM 1993 - DATE

An Act of Parliament in 1958 created the Folk Museum, though the open air museum at Cultra was not opened until 1964. In 1967 the Ulster Folk Museum merged with the Belfast Transport Museum to become the Ulster Folk and Transport Museum. However, it was not until 1993 that the dedicated buildings housing the road and rail exhibits were opened. They were expanded in 1998. There is an extensive collection of horse and electric tramcars, which are outside the purview of this book. The museum does have three of the ex-County Donegal diesel and petrol railcars. These are the first petrol railcar for the County Donegal Railway, number 1 built in 1905; the diesel locomotive 'Phoenix' (originally a steam tram locomotive on the Clogher Valley Railway); and the final vehicle is the first articulated diesel railcar to run on Irish rails.

The County Donegal Railway diesel locomotive, formerly a Clogher Valley Railway steam locomotive.

PARRY PEOPLE MOVERS 1993 - DATE

John Parry of Parry People Movers Ltd, formed a Company in 1992 to develop a hybrid drive light rail passenger vehicle using an energy store system. In 1993 a demonstration line was built in Himley Park, near Dudley, as a pleasure ride for visitors. This also formed an experimental platform for the further development of a flywheel drive vehicle. Initially the concept was for the flywheel to be driven by an electric motor. When the tram stopped to allow passengers to alight and board it would be at a point where it connected to an electricity supply. This powered the electric motor that speeded up the flywheel. The kinetic energy in the flywheel was sufficient to drive the tram around the whole circuit several times. This worked successfully and other trams were built to be taken around the country to demonstrate the system. 1994 saw the concept being demonstrated in Birmingham, Barking, Brighton, Swansea and Bristol.

A number of heritage railways agreed to allow lengthier demonstrations on their lines:

1995 Welshpool and Llanfair Railway
1998 - 2009 Cambian Railways
1998 - 2000 Bristol Harbour Railway
2000 Festiniog Railway
2001 Welsh Highland
2002 and 2003 Severn Valley Railway
2005 Wensleydale Railway
2005 Great Central Railway
2005, 2006 and 2008 Chasewater Railway

Parry People Mover number 139 001 entering Stourbridge Junction Station on its regular service between that station and Stourbridge Town.

A local railway, the Stourbridge Junction to Stourbridge Town line was popular with commuters wanting to reach the main line services to Birmingham and Worcester and with Saturday shoppers. However, demand on Sundays was not sufficient to encourage the rail operator to run a service. In 2002 it was suggested that the Perry People Mover could provide an economic service. It was agreed that there should be a trial service using the Parry vehicle. A car (number 12) was moved to the line in July and used under an engineer's licence (not in public service) while the necessary authority was agreed. This took far longer than had been anticipated. During this time permission was also sought from the authorities to build a light maintenance depot at Stourbridge Junction Station, initially without success. The car was moved back to the Parry works to enable a full inspection to be undertaken (required for the permission and impossible at Stourbridge as there was no pit or equipment to raise the tram). It was anticipated that the formal approval to use the tram would have been granted in 2003. In fact, the procedure was so complex for a vehicle with new and unusual technology that it was not until 11th December 2005 that the public service was able to be started (the official launch was on 5th February 2006). The car used was PPM 50, number 999 900. The People Mover service was a limited experiment only on Sundays, the rest of the week continued to use the heavy rail Class 153 single coach diesel railcar. In 2006 a maintenance and storage depot was built at the end of the line at Stourbridge Junction Station. The experiment ended as scheduled in December 2006.

In June 2007 it was announced that the Government had agreed to operating the Stourbridge branch with People Movers for seven days a week. The service was to start in December 2008 with two new People Movers. The two new People Movers had body frames made by Main Road Sheet Metal in Leyland, the body panels were by Trailways, Bloxwich and chassis from Alan Keef, Ross-on-Wye. The assembly was carried out by Trailways. The cars were classified as Class 139 and given the numbers 139 001 and 139 002. The second car was assembled by Northwest's, Blackburn. The fuel used by the cars is propane gas (LPG) driving a flywheel that drives the wheels through a hydrostatic pump and hydrostatic motors. Testing of the cars was carried out on the Chasewater Heritage Railway. The Stourbridge service started with 139 002 in March 2009. There were some teething problems that took several weeks to resolve, during which time the 153 railcar was used when the Parry car had to be removed for repairs. Car 139 001 arrived on 7th May 2009, while the original car, number 12, was removed for return to Cradley Heath. The full public service started on 22nd June 2009 with both vehicles available. Normally the service is operated by one car, with the other in reserve. The limited passenger capacity is off-set by running a much more frequent service, with a trip every ten minutes, compared to the previous fifteen-minute service. Demonstrations of other Parry People Movers have continued with car 12 being used on the Mid Hants Railway.

The Sheffield Supertram system's newest road-rail multicar vehicle. Photograph Peter Huxford.

SHEFFIELD SOUTH YORKSHIRE SUPERTRAM 1994 – DATE

The Supertram in Sheffield opened to the public in 1994 and for the opening it purchased a road-rail lorry with a lifting platform to enable the engineers to get access to the overhead for repairs and maintenance. The registration number is M992 NNB and it was made by Multicar and has an Iveco F1C 3 ltr diesel engine. Multicar is the trade name for these vehicles that are manufactured by HakoGmbh, Bad Oldesloe, Germany. A second road-rail Multicar was purchased in 2002 (registration number YM02 DJY) as the tramway system had expanded. Both are currently in use.

FINTOWN RAILWAY 1995 – c2010

There are two groups in Ireland focused on the preservation of the 3ft. gauge Donegal Railways. One has a length of track running from Fintown Station with the Comhlacht Traenach na Gael-tachta Lair operating as a heritage railway. In 1995, in order to operate a service, a Simplex 102T diesel shunter (with a Deutz F6L912 Diesel engine) was acquired with the three Charleroi tram trailers that were redundant from the Shane's Castle railway. The railway gives short trips with the shunter hauling one, two or three tram trailers, depending on the passenger numbers. The railway also has an ex-Bord na Mona Ruston diesel locomotive.

The three ex-Charleroi trailers on the Fintown Railway. Two have been repainted in Donegal livery while that on the right still has its Shane's Castle colours.

The ex-Donegal railcoach runs along Loch Finn paired with the Simplex locomotive.

In 2004 the line was loaned the Donegal Railway railcoach number 18, that had been restored in 1996 by the North West of Ireland Railway Society. The railcoach runs back to back with the Simplex locomotive to give visitors rides along the line (reminiscent of the practices of Col. Stephens). A refurbished bogie carriage arrived in 2007, it had also run on Shane's Castle Railway. This carriage had been adapted for wheelchair access to enable disabled passengers to travel. The three tram trailers were now surplus and were offered for sale. One was purchased by the Southwold Railway Trust and it made the return trip to England and is in storage. It is believed that the other two trailers were purchased by private individuals. The tramway operates only in the Summer season from June to September.

UPPER DOUGLAS CABLE TRAMWAY 1996 – c1998

There have been some rather strange examples of the internal combustion engine being used on tramways in the British Isles, but this is probably the strangest. It features a bungalow that was an amalgam of two cable trams that were joined to make the restored car that then ran on an operating public horse tramway while propelled by a diesel Land Rover. The story starts with the demise of the Upper Douglas Cable Tramway on 19th August 1929. This left 16 cable trams with no job to do. An enterprising local, Charles McArten, purchased all of them as a scheme to convert them into holiday bungalows. The idea being to put them in pairs, side by side, to make a single bungalow, surprisingly still on their bogies. Astonishingly, a pair, numbers 72 and 73, survived in this condition for almost 40 years. In 1968 they were purchased by enthusiasts and it proved possible to reconstruct one complete car from the two bodies and mechanical parts. The reconstruction was completed in 1976 and the car was moved to the horse tram depot. At first it

Upper Douglas Cable Tramway car number 73 (the other end is 72) is pushed for an Enthusiasts' special.

appeared that the restored tramcar would remain a static exhibit, there being no cable track. However, the cable track had the same 3ft. gauge as the horse tramway. It was decided that in 1976 it should take part in the procession to celebrate the centenary of the opening of the horse tramway. The lack of propulsion was solved by using a Land Rover to push the car along the promenade track. This proved a success and so popular that various Land Rovers were hired to provide a service of special trips for enthusiasts to ride on the cable car once more. This continued until 1995. In 1996 the car was converted to battery operation with electric motors powering the bogies. This meant it no longer needed a Land Rover and the sight of the tramcar running by itself along the promenade was far more appealing to visitors. In 2010 the Jurby Transport Museum was opened and the cable car was moved in as an exhibit and it continues to remain at the museum.

MIDLAND METRO 1999—DATE

The first ancillary vehicle to be used on the Midland Metro was an overhead inspection road/rail lorry registration number Q204 HFR. Built by Brecknell Willis, it is believed that the lorry was acquired in 1999 during the building of the tramway and kept to assist in the maintenance and repairs on the overhead. The Metro did have a number of problems with its overhead that took a while to resolve. It continued to give service until the Unimog was purchased in 2004. The Brecknell Willis vehicle was sold to Blackpool Tramway in 2005, where it continues to give service.

No photograph of Q204 HFR while at the Midland Metro has been found, this shows it in Blackpool after having been sold to the seaside tramway.

The Midland Metro rail mounted scissors lifting platform.

The Midland Metro Unimog undertaking clearance testing on new track. Photograph Peter Huxford.

There is also a specialist road/rail lifting platform vehicle that is thought to have been part of the maintenance fleet since the opening of the tramway. This carries the number 08 and is registered as R610 NMJ. It works in conjunction with a rail mounted scissors lifting platform, though it is not known when this joined the fleet.

The newest works lorry is a road/rail Unimog (registration number Q179 VOH) that joined the tramway in 2004 and is still in use.

NOTTINGHAM EXPRESS TRANSIT 2002—DATE

The official opening of the Nottingham Express Transit system was on 8th March 2004, following extensive testing and 'shadow running'. As was usual with the new generation of tramways being built in Britain, the construction was achieved by contractors using engineering vehicles, including many that could run on road or rail. The tramway had purchased a Unimog in 2002 for

The Nottingham Transit Unimog has a variety of different types of equipment. Here the lifting arm has been fitted with a platform for working on the overhead.

their own use and this was kept busy in the lead-up to the opening to the public. The vehicle chosen was a multi-purpose unit, registration number FG52 WCC. It was able to be fitted with a lifting platform, a snow plough or a winch. It had a small low sided wagon body for carrying parts, and rubber tyres for road use, while when required to run on rails it had small flanged steel wheels that could be lowered to guide the vehicle, the drive coming from the rubber wheels running along the top of the rails. The Unimog continues to give service on the tramway.

Nottingham has also had an interesting arrangement with the Sheffield Stagecoach Supertram system. Two ancillary road-rail vehicles from Sheffield (with accompanying maintenance staff) were used on the Nottingham system at various times. These were the Multicar and Iveco maintenance vehicles. These were in addition to a variety of other road-rail maintenance vehicles brought in by contractors for working on specific contracts.

VOLK'S ELECTRIC RAILWAY 2004 - DATE

Over the many years of its existence the Volk's Railway has undergone significant change, maintenance and rebuilding. All this had been done using the existing fleet. However, in 2004 it was decided to purchase a dedicated works car that was diesel powered, so it could be operated whether the line was under power or not. A second hand Simplex diesel works locomotive was purchased. It was the last locomotive to be ordered from Motor Rail Limited, as soon after the order was placed, the Company was acquired by Alan Keef Limited in 1987. The Volk's locomotive (works number 40SD530 with a Perkins engine) was built in 1988 for Butterley Brick Company Limited. When the Brickworks closed in 1991 the locomotive was returned to Alan Keef, who overhauled it and offered it for sale. The Volk's Railway purchased it in 2004 and it was taken to Brighton to be used for inspection and maintenance.

The second hand Simplex diesel purchased by the Volk's Electric Railway in 2004, the first non-electric vehicle on the railway.

Ex-Croydon Tramlink number 058 at Crich towing Johannesburg 60.

CROYDON TRAMLINK 2006 - 2010

Croydon Tramlink was officially opened on the morning of 10th May 2000 with rides for officially invited guests. In the afternoon the public were allowed to ride on the trams free of charge, with the public paying service commencing the following day. It was not until 2006 that the system acquired diesel engine vehicles when two DB class Klv 53 engineer's rail crane, four-wheel, powered works cars were purchased second hand from the German state railway Deutsche Bahn. They had been made by Sollinger Hütte in 1978. In addition, three matching four-wheel trucks were also purchased. The rail cranes were numbered 058 and 059 and the trucks 060, 061 and 062. Deutsche Bahn had begun purchasing this type of maintenance vehicle from 1964 and eventually had a fleet of 840 of them. As they became surplus to requirements they were sold off to other railways and tramways and so Tramlink purchased them for general maintenance work. By 2009 there was no longer any need for them and they were offered for sale. Rail crane 058 and truck 061 were purchased by the National Tramway Museum and they arrived at the museum on 19th January 2010. Rail crane 059 and trucks 060 and 062 were sold to the Rushden Transport Museum in March 2010.

JURBY TRANSPORT MUSEUM 2010 – DATE

The Jurby Transport Museum on the Isle of Man opened in 2010 in a hanger on the disused airfield of RAF Jurby. The airfield was opened in 1939 and closed in 1963. Since then it has had various uses, but the interest for this book is the Jurby Transport Museum. It has a free entry and in the collections are the petrol locomotive 'Planet', its carriage from the Queen's Pier at Ramsey and the Upper Douglas cable car. All are static displays.

GIANT'S CAUSEWAY AND BUSHMILLS RAILWAY 2010 - DATE

The town of Portrush is a few miles from the town of Bushmills, renowned for its distillery and the Giant's Causeway. In 1887 a 3ft. gauge tramway was built to connect Portrush with the Causeway, to enable visitors to the area to travel easily to see the natural wonder of the famous rock formations. The line ran mainly on its own right of way alongside the road. Initially the tramway used hydro-electricity to power the tramcars using a third rail collection system, except in the town of Portrush where there was street running and a live third rail would have been dangerous. Here steam tram locomotives were used to haul the tramcars and their trailers. Later the electricity was supplied via an overhead wire and so the electric cars could be driven into the town. The line ran until it was closed in 1949.

The growing popularity of the area prompted a group to set up the Giant's Causeway & Bushmills Railway to develop a line on the old track bed between the western side of Bushmills and the Causeway. The line opened in 2002 using two steam locomotives, and two diesel locomotives (an ex-Bord na Mona Barclay and a Simplex 'T' Class) plus carriages, all from the old Shane's Castle railway. These ran a popular service, but did not represent the history of the line. In 2010 the company purchased three carriages and a diesel locomotive designed and built by Severn Lamb UK Limited, using the original electric cars and trailers as inspiration. The locomotive was designed to have the outward appearance of one of the original electric tramcars and it, and the carriages, are painted in a livery similar to the original trams. The power for the diesel tram is a Kubota V3600-E3 engine and its internal combustion origins are evident by the diesel filling cap on one side. The tramway stock is regularly used with the steam locomotives only being used occasionally.

The diesel locomotive on the Giant's Causeway and Bushmills Railway takes its design from the original electric tramcars that ran nearly 70 years ago. This replica tramcar is given away by its diesel tank refill cap and the fact that it does not carry any passengers.

RUSHDEN TRANSPORT MUSEUM 2010 – DATE

The remaining works vehicles from Croydon Tramlink, crane car 059 and trucks 060 and 062 were purchased by Rushden Transport Museum, Northamptonshire and moved to the museum site. They are being used as engineer's vehicles for the maintenance and development of the site.

Ex-Croydon works car number 059 at Rushden Transport Museum. Photograph Roger Monk.

DUBLIN LUAS 2011 - DATE

The Dublin light railway system, Luas, opened to public traffic in 2004. In 2009 the operators of the system, Alstom, concluded that a track cleaning vehicle was required. An advertisement was placed inviting companies to put forward proposals to meet the need for a vehicle that could operate on roadway and reserved track and clean the track and surrounding areas. The contract was won by Holden Plant Rentals Limited of Mullinavat, Co. Kilkenny. The vehicle was built by Schorling Rail Tech Gmbh, Hannover. It has a Mercedes Benz Axor 1833 two-axle truck chassis and the registration number H 041205. As well as two rotary brushes it has water jets for cleaning the rail groove and vacuum hoses to collect the dirty water in an on-board tank. It has a two axle bogie fitted between the front and rear road axles. To work on the sections of reserved track the bogie is lowered, raising the road wheels. The rail axles are powered by a hydrostatic drive. It is road legal, but when running on the rail wheels it has the tramway track signalling equipment enabling it to safely run on the track between operating tramcars.

The Schorling track cleaning road-rail lorry on the Dublin Luas. Photograph: Holden Plant Rentals

The multi-use Unimog purchased by the new Edinburgh Tramway. Here it demonstrates some of the many different types of equipment that it has to assist in the maintenance of the tramway, although the pantograph is a bit of a surprise.

EDINBURGH TRAMWAY 2014 - DATE

The Edinburgh tramway chose to purchase just one ancillary vehicle, however, it is a fleet of vehicles in itself. Ordered in 2010 it was not used for four years, while the delayed tramway was finishing its construction. Indeed, it was displayed by Mercedes Benz at the Innotrans Exhibition in Germany in 2010 – 2011. It was delivered to Edinburgh and was ready for the opening of the tramway in 2014. The road-rail vehicle is a Unimog with a 4.8 litre four-stroke diesel engine and it has eight forward gears and six reverse gears and a massive 145 litre fuel tank. It consists of a basic lorry base with additional equipment including a lifting platform and a water tank for washing the groove in the track. It can also be fitted with a snow plough and a winch, truly making it a multipurpose engineer's vehicle. There is also a low sided road-rail trailer. Unfortunately, the vehicle was itself the cause of delaying the tram service when it broke down on the track in February 2017. The Edinburgh tramway also saw another rail maintenance vehicle on its system when a contractor's rail grinder was used to remove some track corrugations.

FURTHER READING

CROYDON TRAMLINK

Tramlink, Official Handbook: by Micheal Steward, John Gent and Colin Stannard, published by Capital Transport, 2000.
Croydon's Transport Through the Ages: published by CNHSS The Croydon Natural History and Scientific Society, 2001.

MANX ELECTRIC RAILWAY

Isle of Man Railways Fleet List 2nd Edition: by Barry Edwards, published by B & C Publications, 1997.
Isle of Man Railways Locomotive, Tram and Rolling Stock Directory: by Barry Edwards, published by B & C Publications, 1999.

SHANE'S CASTLE RAILWAY, NORTHERN IRELAND

http://www.bbc.co.uk/history/domesday/dblock/NI-308000-387000/page/3
http://www.geograph.org.uk/snippet/8686

TYNE AND WEAR METRO

Suburban Railways of Tyneside: by Alan Young, published by Martin Bairstow, 1999.
20 Years of the Tyne and Wear Metro: by Geoffrey Skelsey, Tramways and Urban Transit, June, July, August 2000.

SOUTHEND PIER

The Longest Pier in the World: by Peggy Dowie and Ken Crowe, published by Friends of Southend Pier Museum, 1987.
Southend Pier Railway: by K. A. Frost and D. J. Carson, published by Ian Henry Publications, 1990.
Southend-on-Sea Pier, The Longest Pleasure Pier in the World: published by The Leisure Services Department Southend-on-Sea Borough Council, 1996.
Pier Railways and Tramways of the British Isles, 2nd Edition: by Keith Turner, published by The Oakwood Press, 1999
The Railway to the End of the Longest Pleasure Pier in the World: by John Stevenson, The Narrow Gauge No. 168, Spring 2000.
A Brief History of Southend Pier: published by Leisure, Culture and Amenity Services Department Southend-on-Sea Borough Council, 2002.

DOCKLANDS LIGHT RAILWAY

Docklands Light Railway, Official Handbook 1st Edition: by Stephen Jolly and Bob Bayman, published by Capital Transport, 1987.
Docklands Light Railway, Official Handbook 2nd Edition: by Bob Bayman and Stephen Jolly, published by Capital Transport, 1988.

BLACKPOOL NORTH PIER

Blackpool North Pier Tramway: by Alison Orchard, published by Lancastrian Transport Publications, 1992.
Pier Railways and Tramways of the British Isles, 2nd Edition: by Keith Turner, published by The Oakwood Press, 1999
http://www.citytransport.info/B-Pier.htm

MANCHESTER METROLINK

Metrolink Official Handbook: by Eric Ogden and John Senior, published by Transport Publishing Company, 1991.
Metrolink: by John Senior and Eric Ogden, published by Transport Publishing Company, 1992.

DOUGLAS HORSE TRAMWAY

http://www.britishtramsonline.co.uk.

PARRY PEOPLE MOVERS

http://www.parrypeoplemovers.com/

FINTOWN RAILWAY

http://www.antraen.com/

UPPER DOUGLAS CABLE TRAMWAY

Double Century: by Stan Bassett and Keith Pearson, published by Adam Gordon, 1996

NOTTINGHAM EXPRESS TRANSIT

Nottingham's New Trams, The NET Success Story: by Geoffrey Skelsey, published by LRTA.

VOLK'S ELECTRIC RAILWAY

http://volkselectricrailway.co.uk/
Motor Rail Ltd: by Alan Keef, published by Lightmoor Press, 2016

NATIONAL TRAMWAY MUSEUM, CRICH

https://en.wikipedia.org/wiki/List_of_tramcars_of_the_National_Tramway_Museum

RUSHDEN TRANSPORT MUSEUM

http://rhts.co.uk/

DUBLIN LUAS

http://www.irrs.ie/index.htm

EDINBURGH TRAMWAY

http://www.bbc.co.uk/news/uk-scotland-edinburgh-east-fife-27538212
Unimog vehicle to rescue broken down trams: Edinburgh Evening News, 4th March 2014.
http://www.edinburghnews.scotsman.com/news/transport/unimog-vehicle-to-rescue-broken-down-trams-1-3327552?plckOnPage=3

ACKNOWLEDGEMENTS

Writing about tramway history entirely relies on gathering information and there are many sources from people who have recorded events (for examlpe contemporaneous newspapers) through legal documents to system histories. For the most recent tramways I have been fortunate to be able to visit many of the systems and gather information first hand. I am privileged to have a wide circle of friends who share my interest and generously share their knowledge with me. To them all I am immensely grateful. I would like to particularly thank the following who have supported my writing and been patient enough to answer my questions.

Alan Kirkman has helped me in all my writings and his interest in Blackpool tramways has meant I never have to worry about delving into the dark recesses of its history. Roger Monk has a wide interest in tramways and industrial railways. The latter knowledge has been a source I have found invaluable. Roger has also been very generous in sharing his and his late father's collections of transport photographs. John Prentice has a great number of connections through his web site www.tramwayinfo.com (itself a fine source of information on tramways and model tramways) and he is happy to share his knowledge with me. Bob Appleton is the Editor of the Tramway and Light Railway Society magazine 'Tramfare' and helps me with my more convoluted wording as well as sharing his extensive knowledge. Mike Wilson has shared his considerable knowledge of Blackpool's less well known trams and support vehicles (a complex area). I am immensely grateful for all their generous help.

The Edinburgh multi-purpose 'Unimog' service vehicle, showing its wide variety of equipment, including rail cleaning, a crane and a winch. It is also able to carry out snow clearing.

INDEX